★The★
HOLLYWOOD
ASSISTANTS
HANDBOOK

86 Rules for Aspiring Power Players

★The★
HOLLYWOOD ASSISTANTS HANDBOOK

86 Rules for Aspiring Power Players

By Hillary Stamm and Peter Nowalk

WORKMAN PUBLISHING ■ NEW YORK

*To everyone
who's ever answered someone else's phone.*

Library of Congress Cataloging-in-Publication Data
Stamm, Hillary.
Hollywood assistants handbook: 86 rules for aspiring power players / by
Hillary Stamm and Peter Nowalk.
          p. cm.
ISBN 978-0-7611-4746-6 (alk. paper)
1. Motion pictures–Vocational guidance. I. Nowalk, Peter. II. Title.
PN1995.9.P75S72 2007
791.43023–dc22   2007021121

Design by Robb Allen
Illustrated by Tim Bower

Workman books are available at special discounts when purchased in bulk
for premiums and sales promotions as well as for fund-raising or educational
use. Special editions or book excerpts can also be created to specification.
For details, contact the Special Sales Director at the address below.

Workman Publishing Company, Inc.
225 Varick Street
New York, NY 10014-4381
www.workman.com

Printed in U.S.A.

First printing March 2008
10 9 8 7 6 5 4 3 2 1

CONTENTS

TAKE 3: THE SHOOT

TAKE 4: THE RELEASE

TAKE 5: AWARDS SEASON

INTRODUCTION

BASED ON A TRUE STORY . . .

We were you. Yes, just a few years ago, we were you. We had graduated from college, the real world upon us, and our friends were heading off to a variety of bright futures—med school, law school, Peace Corps, consulting firms, Capitol Hill, a year in Europe . . . But then there was us, packing up our family's old Volvo wagon for the glitz and glamour of the Movie Business. If only we knew then what we know now.

Our early days in Hollywood can only be described as a series of misadventures. Crashing on friends' sofas, e-mailing resumes from Kinko's, begging for interviews at the temp agencies . . . "Can you roll 15 calls at once?" the lady asked. "Roll?" we choked. Back then, "nightlife" consisted of going out with this guy that was the son of our mom's hairdresser. While he and his friends from the studio all ordered round after round of drinks, we worried how we'd pay for that one $12 mojito we downed an hour ago. Apartments fell through, roommates ended up being crazy, and the good jobs eluded us. For the first time in our lives, we realized, the paved road had suddenly crumbled. We pondered packing it up. "Maybe grad school's not such a bad idea . . ."

Instead we stayed, eventually using those friends of friends to get jobs in a mailroom (minimum wage now seemed extravagant), which led to the floater assistant gig at the studio, which led to the production company . . . all leading up to the two of us having our "meet cute" on the studio lot. Working as assistants 12 hours a day together—answering phones, fetching coffees, copying scripts that were bound to turn into turkeys onscreen—the two of us became good friends. We shared stories of how we arrived at these jobs, laughing at our naïve expectations, cringing over our biggest embarrassments, and always reminding each other not to take it all so seriously.

The lessons contained in this book are a result of these many years we've worked as assistants. We've seen it all: big companies, small companies, amazing bosses and, well, not so amazing bosses. We mastered the phones, memorized the schedules, and put up with the abuses because we knew that in order to make it in this business we had to *learn by doing*. So that's what we did. We stepped into the mud pit that is Hollywood, rolled around in it, and let it soak into every pore. Now it's your turn to learn from our mistakes.

Trust us, we would have killed for a book like this to read on the ride out to L.A., or on our friend's futon in Beverlywood adjacent. Eventually we figured it out though, and you will too. Hell, in just a few years you'll even have your *own* assistant. Just don't, whatever you do, touch the celebrities.

FADE IN

Welcome, friends, and congratulations. You are about to embark on a journey of incredible wealth, international fame, and record-breaking success. It won't be long before you're jet-setting to St. Tropez with celebutantes and accepting back-to-back Best Picture Oscars. Don't forget to thank Mom . . .

Okay, that's a lie. If only it were that easy. The real? Starting off any new job is hard. Whether selling widgets in Wisconsin or politicking in D.C. or answering phones in Hollywood, you are going to need help navigating the shark-infested waters that are the real world. What better way to prepare than to learn the lessons needed to make it in the *most* shark-infested industry—the movie business.

Now some of you've bought this book because you know deep within your soul that you're the next Steven Spielberg. Others are reading this because *US Weekly* is your bible and you're dying to know what Julia Roberts' assistant's life is like behind the glossy photos. Then there's the last group of you—those who have no desire whatsoever to work in Hollywood but know that the lessons learned here can be applied anywhere. (It was either buy this or that book on *How to Be an Accounting All-Star,* and well, this seemed a bit more interesting.)

No matter what your reason may be, you are to be congratulated for now being one step ahead of the game. Nicely done, friend. But enough with the self-congratulatory pats on the back. There's work to do . . .

What you're about to read is more than a book. It's a way of life. The following pages contain every frothy tidbit and dirty secret you'll need to survive—*and* thrive—in Hollywood. Think about it as your very own extreme career makeover. By embracing the whole new attitude, personal mantra, and holy religion we've mapped out here, we're going to mold you into one successful Future Power Player, my friend.

Why is all of this necessary? Because without paying attention to and then implementing everything you're about to learn in this book, you will end up a failure, more likely to work the counter at the Cineplex than have your own movies watched there. "Would you like to upgrade that popcorn to a jumbo and add a frosty beverage for a dollar more?" There. Did we scare you?

As you're about to learn, in the movie business, as in all business, whom you work for is as important as who you are. In order to get anywhere as an assistant—that is to say, a future executive, agent, producer, etc.—you will be forced to buy into this system. So, yes, you were once the go-to auteur at Uni and won Best Short at your local film festival. But now you're a professional secretary, spending every waking hour of your life slaving away for the sake of someone else's career.

We're not sure who exactly dreamt up this system. Well, we can't answer for sure, but we do know that it was a very long time ago, medieval in fact, when some blacksmith in a barn decided he needed cheap help if he was going to get all those spears done in time for the battle. What he came up with was something called the apprentice.

"I've seen that show!"

We're not talking about Donald Trump. You see, Hollywood is one of the last true *apprentice industries.* Whenever an agent makes a deal, a studio head green-lights a movie, or the red carpet's unfurled at the glitzy world premiere of *Snow Dogs 8: Canines Take the Caribbean,* it's assistants that made it possible. Without us, phones would go unanswered, meetings would never happen, and celebrities would have to walk their own dogs. In other words, the town would crumble.

Now for the part that's hard to swallow. Everyone looking to break into the Biz—rich, poor, brilliant, or banal—has to start out in the same place: the bottom. Even the most successful producers, executives, and agents in Hollywood began their careers sending faxes, scheduling car washes, and fighting with copiers. Sure, nepotism may get your foot in the door, but that door always opens onto a cubicle. Good thing your wise elders are here.

Just like the journey a movie makes from the page to silver screen, the rough draft that is you (yes, we know you were BMOC at Northwestern) is about to begin the long process of becoming a future somebody. Hence, without further ado . . .

(Yes, now is when you turn the page.)

TAKE 1: DEVELOPMENT

IN THE MINDS OF EXECUTIVES EVERYWHERE, DEVELOPMENT IS THE process by which studios and producers turn scripts into structurally sound and commercially viable projects. In reality, this never happens. Because what usually occurs during development is one thing and one thing only: scripts get worse. (You've been watching movies lately, right? Enough said.)

Your DEVELOPMENT refers to the earliest stage of your life as an assistant. From that initial inkling to move to Hollywood to the moment before you start your first gig, these lessons will prepare you for the mental and physical challenges of getting settled in your new life. Don't worry, we'll teach you how to have fun too. Can you say free liquor?

"So, let's get this show on the road!"

Hang on, sport. First up, a little test.

"Ew!"

Chill. You should be able to pass this one pretty easily, bucko. As you'll notice throughout the book, we might call you names every so often, to the point where you may start to take offense. Don't. **HPPs** (Hollywood Power Players)* are notorious for their skills at verbal abuse. We're just trying to break you in early. The little test below will reveal where you fall on the Moron Scale—not because we think you're actually a moron, but because we want to determine whether you have what it takes to enter through the fiery gates of Hellywood in the first place. Proceed at your own risk.

HOW TO TELL IF YOU'RE A MORON WHO SHOULD PACK UP THE COROLLA AND MOVE BACK HOME:

Please answer the following questions truthfully and honestly. Cheating, after all, will only prolong your suffering.

1. **True or False:** Executives in Hollywood live a life of glamour and fabulousness.

2. **Pick the one item that you will NOT need as an assistant:**
   a. Driver's license
   b. Headset
   c. Cell phone
   d. Conscience

3. **Which of the following actors will still be starring in movies in the year 2052?**
   a. Ben Affleck
   b. Ryan Gosling
   c. Freddie Prinze Jr.
   d. Mel Gibson

*Not sure of the meaning of words in bold type? Check out the Glossary of Hollywood Lingo on page 193.

4. When asked to "roll calls," you . . .
  a. take the attendance of your coworkers, Marine style.
  b. fall down on the floor and do tumble rolls while telling your boss who called.
  c. start madly dialing all the people your boss owes a phone call.
  d. run up and down the hall asking the other assistants if they know where to get a warm, fluffy, dinner roll.

5. Which of the following will NOT help catapult you to an executive job?
  a. Being an all-star assistant
  b. Reading every script you can get your hands on
  c. Befriending Kate Hudson
  d. Surfing MySpace for the next hot director
  e. None of the above

6. True or False: In general, agents are good people.

7. In which of these neighborhoods would you find the head of a studio at 3 P.M. on a Wednesday?
  a. Van Nuys
  b. Echo Park
  c. Culver City
  d. Santa Clarita

8. You are asked to state your honest-to-god opinion of your boss's most recent movie. You . . .
  a. say you loved it, even though you hated it.
  b. say you hated it.
  c. say you liked it.
  d. avoid the question by pointing out that your boss's mom is holding on line 2.

9. True or False: The most powerful person on the set is the executive producer.

10. Your boss needs a blowout before the premiere. You . . .
  a. bring hairspray and a blow-dryer to work.
  b. get a professional to come to the office at the cost of a small fortune.
  c. book her at Supercuts. It's close to the premiere.
  d. decide her hair looks fine.

Answers:
1. False; **2.** d; **3.** b; **4.** c; **5.** a; **6.** False; **7.** c; **8.** a; **9.** False; **10.** b

How did you do? Oh god, that bad? Well there's always beauty school for you, dropout.

"NOOOOOOOOOOO!!"

Okay, okay. One more chance. Just pay very close attention from here on out. We still have faith in you, babe. Really.

Ditch Your Diploma

"I graduated summa cum laude from Amherst with a bachelor's in Philosophy and minor in Women's Studies."

NO ONE CARES. REALLY. YOU MAY AS WELL JUST get over it now. That impossible Film Semiotics A-minus that you are so proud of? Yes, of no interest. The senior thesis on Class Structure in Elizabethan England that you spent three semesters writing? Nope. Consider it forgotten. So you might as well take that impeccable transcript, douse it in some gasoline, and set it on fire because from here on out no one gives a damn whether or not you went to college, much less what or how you did there.

You may have a bit of an existential crisis here. "But I am too smart for this. How will I take this intellect I've sculpted and perfected for four blissful years and use it to push a mail cart? I could've been president of the law review. Was it all for nothing???"

Yes.

Just kidding. Your education will actually end up being useful in ways that you'd least expect. That class you took for one unit in speed-reading? Beyond helpful when you're confronted with the stacks of screenplays your boss will soon make you read for her. That history presentation you gave on the Boston Tea Party? You'll be so glad you kept your notes when Brian Grazer decides to develop the movie. The Calculus 7 seminar you scored a B-plus in? Truly necessary for computing your boss's expenses during that five-day, twelve-country European *X-Men 3* tour. Ridiculous? Yes. Necessary? Quite.

Point is, even if it's not your academic knowledge that you'll be using, surviving in the Biz will certainly require one thing no college student goes without: diligence. So take that work ethic you fine-tuned for all those years in college and apply it to your new life. You will need to churn out the long hours, read a zillion scripts, and show up the next day thrilled about doing it all again. Energy, chutzpah, and perseverance are going to be the keys to snagging that corner office, not your extensive knowledge of Nietzsche's early essays.

★ *Tarantino's college–the video store.*

HOLLYWOOD HIGH:
THEY WORKED HARD FOR THEIR MONEY

What better way to prove our point than to do a small survey of our favorite HPPs and their respective educational experience. We asked ourselves, "What's Oprah's alma mater? Did Jerry Bruckheimer spend his Saturday nights at Uni memorizing the periodic table?" As you'll see from the list we've compiled below, it wasn't solely studying that got these HPPs to where they are today.

CONNECT THE DOTS:

1. Sofia Coppola
Writer/Director

A. Tennessee State University. Was a news anchor for CBS while taking classes.

2. Quentin Tarantino
Writer/Director

B. Dropped out of Cal State Long Beach, applied to USC film school twice but was never admitted.

3. Stacey Snider
Chairman of DreamWorks

C. Attended University of Arizona, moved to New York and got a job in an advertising agency mailroom, which launched him into producing TV commercials.

4. Steve Jobs
CEO of Apple, Pixar

D. Dropped out of UT- Austin to get a job in the William Morris mailroom.

5. Oprah Winfrey
Talk Show Host/Mogul

E. Attended Mills College and the California Institute of the Arts.

6. Ron Meyer
CEO of Universal

F. Served in the Marine Corps, then was a short order cook before becoming a messenger at an agency.

7. David Geffen
CEO of DreamWorks

G. Dropped out of Reed College but continued to audit classes like Calligraphy.

8. Jerry Bruckheimer
Film & TV Producer

H. Went to University of Pennsylvania, then UCLA Law School, then worked in an agency mailroom.

9. Steven Spielberg
Director/Studio Chief

I. Dropped out of high school, worked in a video store, and acted in shows like *The Golden Girls.*

Answers:
1. E; **2.** I; **3.** H; **4.** G; **5.** A; **6.** F; **7.** D; **8.** C; **9.** B

Put the Fantasy on Hold

"I want to produce my first movie by 25, direct by 30, and have a house in the Hamptons and a villa on Lake Como not long after. Isn't Hollywood just like so much fun??"

YOU JUST *HAVE* TO WORK IN HOLLYWOOD. Movies are your passion. You grew up watching *It's a Wonderful Life* with your grandmother every Christmas and named your first dog George Bailey. *Kramer vs. Kramer* was the first movie that captured the angst you felt about your parents' divorce. *Willy Wonka and the Chocolate Factory* still speaks to your inner child. Okay, okay, we get it.

You came out here to make movies that you believe in, movies that matter, movies that change the world. Someone has to produce the award-winning movie about Darfur, after all. Why not you?

"Look, kids," you'll tell your own grandkids someday, "that's my name up on that screen." To which they'll respond, "Sweet. *Darfurious* is dope, Pops."

Just a tip: This won't happen. Not right away, at least.

As far as we're concerned, your life is going to be much easier the sooner you get real. Okay, *someday*—you know, about 20 or 25 years from now—you'll be able to make your dreams come true. But for now, today, you have to suck it up and know that your new assistant gig has little to do with your passion for movies.

You see, there is a difference between *thinking* big and *doing* big. Yes, we encourage you to dream the impossible dream. However, chances are you are reading this book right now because you are young and have a lot to learn. A lot. Maybe you think you can win an Oscar next year because "like I really believe in this script." Or maybe you don't think you have to worry about a little thing like a movie's commercial viability.

"Who cares if it makes money? We'll have told my grandmother's life story, and for that I'll get a lifetime of personal fulfillment." Great, go tell it to the loan officer ready to foreclose on the convertible you just bought. Or maybe you think your god-given talent makes you immune to failure, no matter how many bridges you burn or martinis you sip. Oh, you little egomaniac, you.

Our advice? Focus on the immediate. Whether that's getting your foot in the door, procuring a paying job at a studio rather than The Grove,* or getting your boss a ticket to the oversold Sundance buzz-movie, you must take things one step at a time. So rather than continue the delusion that Hollywood can foster art—this is a *business*, remember—accept reality and start treating this assistant life as a JOB. The important stuff—family, true love, a sense of meaning in your life—you'll have to find that later. When? You'll just have to keep reading.

---

*You're new to town, huh? Well, The Grove (189 The Grove Drive; www.thegrovela.com) is only the most hip-happening outdoor mall in all of L.A.—Disneyland for adults, basically. Especially at Christmas, when the hot elves and the faux snow come out.

Network Is Your New Middle Name

"We're not just coming to Hollywood to break in. We're coming to break the door DOWN, baby!"

YOU AND YOUR BEST FRIEND HAVE JUST road-tripped all the way from Ohio with the VW Jetta packed to the brim and visions of champagne and caviar dancing in your head. Your BFF Mandy is going to be an extra until someone notices she's the next Rachel McAdams, while you're going to be the next Scorsese and rock everyone with your brilliant art house film about female empowerment in a small Sudanese village.

Slow down. Before you swagger on stage to accept that Oscar, you're going to want to brush up on what is known as the **informational meeting.** Yes, you're going to want to call up every person you know in this town and set up a time to talk to them. That includes the line producer you met in the Coffee Bean, your uncle's friend who edits trailers for all of Jerry Bruckheimer's flicks, and that chick from high school who supposedly dated Jon Stewart.

It may not seem worthwhile right now, but these are the same people who may be able to recommend you for that dream job later. The more you learn about the various facets of the Biz by taking the time to meet **FOFs** (Friends of Friends) the better off you will be in the long run. Sure Jason's friend Cassy seems like a snot, but she works for the president of production at Buena Vista (that's Disney, in case you didn't know, sport). So ask her out for coffee already. You never know when that huge opportunity is right around the corner, and it's hard to find the time if you're too busy drafting your Best Director acceptance speech.

What do you do in the meeting? Ask questions. Lots and lots of questions, most of which should revolve around the person with whom you're meeting. Everyone likes to talk about themselves, after all. You'll get your chance one day.

★ *Collect digits like you're playing the lotto.*

NETWORK 101

Don't know anyone, you say? Fine, here are other ways to network:

■ **Alumni networks.**
You've already contacted every HPP that went to your college, right? Please say yes. If your college isn't as well organized as some others, steal info from the ones that are (e.g., Wisconsin's helpful website: www.hollywoodbadgers.com).

■ **Hollywood Creative Directory.**
Hunker down for the night with a classic movie (*Metropolis* for all those that slept through Film 101), and write blind letters to all of the execs, agents, and producers you admire. Sure, it's unlikely you'll get a response, but you'd be surprised what sucking up will get you in Hollywood. In this case, a sit-down meeting. (www.hcdonline.com; there's also a good job board on here, folks.)

■ **Temp agencies.**
The filter for all Hollywood jobs, these headhunters will provide you with more information than you could ever want. They'll also help you decide if an agency, production company, or studio sounds like the right fit for you. Here are some places to start:

www.corestaff.com	www.spherion.com
www.adecco.com	www.comaragency.com
www.appleone.com	www.friedmanpersonnel.com

It's Called a Job HUNT for a Reason

"Hi, this is Henry Tisberry calling again. I know, you think I'm weird, calling three times in the past half hour, but this job, like it's the perfect position for me . . . Hello? Is anyone there?"

FINDING YOUR FIRST JOB WILL BE EASY. At any one time there are thousands of entry-level positions open and there won't be nearly enough people applying for them. You are in the driver's seat finally, so sit back and relax and just wait for H.R. to offer you the gig. Salary not big enough? Fine, just ask for more!

Okay, we're lying. For every crappy job there are 50 overqualified applicants willing to kill one another for an interview. (Do you think all those MBAs *want* to sort mail for a living?) The excess of young people in this town will never change. You've chosen a line of work that is beyond attractive to ambitious tykes just dying for a chance in the spotlight.

"But how do I stand out from the crowd?" Simple. Whore yourself.

For starters, you might need to actively try and be in the right place at the right time. I know it's hard to believe, but you will *not* find a job sitting at home watching Barbara and the girls on *The View*.

Not getting any calls about the resume you sent to Universal? Then fill out an application to be a tour guide at the theme park. As an employee of the corporation, you'll be more likely to be hired for that job in the production department than someone not in their ranks. (Case in point, Steven Spielberg interned there early on in his career.) Dying to get a job in the mailroom at William Morris? Become a barista at the nearby Starbucks. You'll have face-to-face contact with every agent coming in for his morning fix. ("Extra hot nonfat with a dollop of foam and I heard you're looking for an assistant . . .") Wondering how to meet the director you want to **P.A.** for? Start selling cars at the Porsche dealership where his entourage hangs out.

It's okay to take a crappy job if there's even a 1 percent chance of meeting someone who will recommend you to a friend who dates the exec who just hired the writer you heard is looking for an assistant. So bring on the shopgirl gig, the Xerox repairman stint, or the cocktail waitress double shift at Hooters because you never know who you're going to meet. The one job we won't allow you to take? Stripper. No one becomes a CEO by dancing on poles.

WHERE TO BEGIN

Not sure where to apply? Sit yourself down in front of the computer and check out these companies. Any of them would be a great place to start off your Hollywood career.

- **Disney**
  www.disney.com

- **Fox Studios**
  www.foxmovies.com

- **Paramount Pictures**
  www.paramount.com

- **Sony**
  www.sonypictures.com

- **Universal**
  www.universalstudios.com

- **Warner Brothers**
  www.warnerbros.com

- **CBS**
  www.cbs.com

- **NBC**
  www.nbc.com

- **Creative Artists Agency**
  www.caa.com

- **United Talent Agency**
  www.unitedtalent.com

- **William Morris Agency**
  www.wma.com

- **Writers Guild of America**
  www.wga.org

- **International Creative Management**
  www.icm.com

- **Endeavor Talent Agency**
  Sorry, but they're too cool to have a dot com

TRICKS TO FIND YOURSELF IN THE RIGHT PLACE AT THE RIGHT TIME

Don't tell anyone, but we're going to actually take a page from a character in Hollywood known as the Wannabe Actor. Namely, his knack for working jobs that put him in the right place at the right time. Here's our guide to minimum-wage workplaces that could put you in front of some HPPs.

Beverly Hills — **Neiman Marcus, Barneys, Bergdorf's**: The only place for HPPs to shop. **Cut**: $100 steaks are meant only for the VIPs. **Nate-N-Al's Diner**: Famous down-home power spot.

Century City — Anywhere in the **Century City Mall**: **MGM, CAA,** and **ICM** are right next door.

Hollywood — **Chateau Marmont**: Cozy chic, plus good for star sightings. **Sky Bar**: Because you have to be on the list. **Concession Stand at the Hollywood Bowl**: HPPs don't have time to whip up a gourmet picnic basket.

West Hollywood	**Pinkberry Frozen Yogurt:** Wait in line with Mischa. **Dan Tana's:** Star sightings for over 40 years. **Joan's on Third:** We would eat here every day if we could.
The Valley	Lot work **(Warner Brothers, Disney, Universal):** Directors, producers, actors: you'll interact with them all. **Tokyo Delve's:** Part sushi, part frat party.
Westside	**Ivy at the Shore:** Delectable home cooking for all the Westside HPPs. **The Viceroy:** Santa Monica's very own Hollywood scene. **Shutters:** Pretend you're in Nantucket with the rest of the Richie Riches. **The Jonathan Club:** Run into HPPs on the beach.
Catering	**Along Came Mary:** Register on their staff to work all the big L.A. premieres, weddings, and bar mitzvahs (www.alongcamemary.com).
Everywhere	**YogaWorks, Equinox, Starbucks:** Top Hollywood obsessions.

There Is No Magic Job List

YOU'VE PROBABLY HEARD OF THE **UTA JOB LIST** (UNITED TALENT Agency, but you knew that). Renowned in assistant and nonassistant circles alike, the **Job List** (J.L.) is a document that catalogs every available job in the entertainment industry, from **C.E.** (Creative Executive) gigs at studios to internships at B-movie labs in Encino. Now, there was a point where this list was actually helpful to **FHPPs** (Future Hollywood Power Players). Unfortunately, as with leg warmers and Jazzercise, that time has passed.

"My older brother swears by the J.L., though. He even got his first job working for Joel Silver off it!" And I'm sure he did . . . about ten years ago.

In the beginning, the thing that made the UTA Job List valuable was that it was hard to get. You actually had to know someone at UTA, and only then could you get hold of this superconfidential document. It was then that the list included things like "Assistant to Cameron Crowe Needed," or "Top Studio CEO Needs Savvy Assistant," and they were all true! These days, Cameron Crowe wouldn't be caught dead having his name on the list.

You see, everyone and her mother has heard about the J.L., and everyone and *his* mother can get a copy in about three minutes flat. For every decent job that ends up listed, there are about 3,000 other people just like you sending their resume. So unless you're one of the first 100 movers and shakers to e-mail off that cover letter, your resume is going in the trash bin. And forget about the listings that are over a day old. Sure, they may say "unfilled," but more often than not this just means that someone at UTA got too lazy to go through and delete the old postings.

Our final word: Sure, get the J.L. Maybe even apply for a few jobs you find there. But whatever you do, do not think that this is all you have to do to find a gig. Otherwise your unemployment is going to last longer than you'd like. We're talking into your thirties.

Instead, what you can try to do is investigate who is in control of compiling the J.L. and then befriend them. How do you do this? Crash their assistant mixer, or hang out at the El Torito across the street from their office, or harass all your FOFs. Just find a way to hear about the jobs long before they hit the J.L. After all, the only gigs that do end up there are the ones that every assistant at UTA and everyone who is friends with an assistant at UTA did not want themselves (21,056 people by our last estimates). In other words, these jobs are pretty lame. Don't be lame.

RESUME POP QUIZ: WHOM WOULD YOU HIRE? Rather than waste energy searching the J.L., here's a better way to use your time—perfecting your resume. Look at these two samples to decipher the difference between a Good Resume and an Evil Resume. Please, please tell us you can figure out which is which.

AL FROMMER
777 Pico Blvd.
Beverlywood, CA 90036

OBJECTIVE: To procure an entry-level position in the entertainment industry.

EDUCATION: Texas Tech, Class of 2007. Double Major in Marketing and Fine Arts.

Too Young?

WORK EXPERIENCE: Red Wagon Entertainment, Los Angeles. Intern. Summers of 2005 and 2006.

- Helped with phones, travel, filing, letter writing, expenses, etc.
- Read and wrote coverage on spec scripts and project samples.
- Proofed creative notes, maintained submission logs, organized weekend read.

Seems to have good experience

Hammers and Hammers Law Firm, Austin, TX. Clerical Secretary. 2004–2005.

- Assisted Partner with office organization.
- Acted as messenger between office and courthouse, averaging 120.3 seconds one way. (Fastest time known to firm.)

Doesn't mind menial work

Olive Garden, Waco, TX. Assistant Manager. 2002–2004.

maybe can have garlic balls at the office?

COMPUTER SKILLS: Proficiency in PCs and Macs: Microsoft Word, Excel, Filemaker Pro, Word Perfect, Netscape, Now-Up-To-Date, Studio System, Final Draft.

Could be a Computer GEEK! Better than a moron

OTHER EXPERIENCE:

Sigma Nu. Social chair two years.

Film Society. Treasurer.

Homeless No More. Volunteered to bring food from dorm dining hall to shelters.

Interested in more than just movie

RESUME #2

RACHEL MANCHESTER
9919 Beverly Glen Blvd.
Beverly Hills, CA 90210

Rich Parents

EDUCATION: Harvard, Class of 2004. Triple major in Biophysics, Philosophy, and Dance.

4.3 GPA (Due to A-plus on honors thesis entitled "Fred Astaire: Anatomy of a Legend.")

Do I care?

WORK EXPERIENCE; Warner Brothers Pictures. Second Assistant to CEO. 2006–2007.

- Responsible for reading all incoming submissions for CEO.

- Proficient in phone sheet, developing big-budget films, and supervising directors on set.

- Single-handedly fixed third-act disaster in *Harry Potter 3* (probably saved studio).

- Tried to convince staff to pass on *Poseidon.* *Bull*

Paramount Pictures. First Assistant to Story Editor. 2004–2005.

- Overhauled entire filing system for the story department (analogous to Dewey decimal system).

- Received Silver Screen Award for Excellence.

Beginning to scare me

OTHER EXPERIENCE:

SAVVY (Saving African Villages Vigorously and Youthfully). Founder and President. 2000–present.

- Received grant from the UN.

- Personally convinced Nelson Mandela and Angelina Jolie to join Board of Directors.

She'll take my job   *THROW IN TRASH!!*

Please note, what you are holding is 100% recycled paper I personally made from old scripts at the studio. Make haste, not waste!

No Pay Is Often the Way

"I worked 12 hours straight and all I get is this free T-shirt?"

SO YOU'VE HIT THE PAVEMENT HARD LOOKING for that big break. But not even the El Pollo Loco across from Sony Pictures is calling you back for an interview, let alone the guy hiring P.A.s for the new *Spider-Man.* "Why, damn it?!!" Well, we can't say for sure, but we think it has something to do with the fact that you didn't do your homework. Instead, you spent your summers in college lying out by your parents' pool and going to keggers with the ol' buddies from Jefferson High.

"I get to be a lazy-ass college student only once," you told yourself. Oh man, were you wrong about that one. Because while you were busy fine-tuning that killer tan, everyone else your age was out interning. That's right—they packed their resumes with summer gigs at production companies, talent agencies, FX labs, and Habitat for Humanity because, "Ya know, I just think it's our duty to give back to the world." In return, they scored assistant jobs right out of college.

No one is going to hire an assistant with no experience. The good news? **Internships** were created for just this reason. I mean, who else is going to work for free but desperate industry wannabes?

We know what you're thinking. You're too old to be an intern. You're too poor to be an intern. You're too qualified to be an intern! None of this is true. You're just *too picky* to be an intern. Here's the thing about being an intern: it will lead to something else. Whether that's another internship or a temp job or a real, live assistant gig with your dream director is up to the Hollygods. What we do know is that, instead of wasting your early days in L.A. sending your resume out for jobs you won't get, you should be meeting as many people as you can. After all, resumes don't hire people. People hire people. The opportunity to meet people could not be more available than through an internship. The fact that you're working for free also encourages your new boss—guilty over your indentured servitude—to go out of his way to find you a job.

Meet Howie. Howie interned at a production company for six weeks, when a second assistant position opened up. The first assistant had a dozen resumes in her fax and no time to interview any of them. So Howie went up to her desk, hit her with an ice-cold Perrier (he knew it was her fave), and it suddenly dawned on her. "Well, he knows his way around the office, I can definitely boss him around, he'll be cheap . . ." Howie was IN, baby! The best part: Now someone serves Howie ice-cold Perriers. See, it pays to suffer.

P.S. As a college grad, you're going to be interning with people *way* younger than thyself. Most likely, they'll be under drinking age and conversations will revolve around the latest PlayStation release. Feel like you'll go ballistic? Ask your supervisor for more work. You'll avoid the kiddie talk and build a reputation as a go-getter.

INTERNING FOR DUMMIES

"QUICK! I need 17 double-sided copies shrunk down to four-by-six for my boss's meeting in five minutes!"

And there you are. In a room the size of a closet with a fancy machine that breaks more frequently than that vintage Mustang you just bought. "What is going on? They said I would take notes, read important scripts . . . Oh no, paper jam in tray 3 again."

Interns, by nature, exist for one reason: to make copies. Here's how not to screw it up:

1. **Count the pages.** As insignificant as this may seem, your script may be going to Russell Crowe in Perth. He may need to read it ASAP if he's going to commit before he starts shooting the *Gladiator* prequel. If page 122—the most suspenseful page in the script—is missing, that's your fault.

2. **Check the draft date.** Great, you paginated perfectly, but it was the *old* draft. Russell's now doubly pissed. Good thing he's too far away to throw a phone at you.

3. **Don't abuse the copier.** It's a given. The $18,000 HP 4000 will break on you. That's no reason to throw a tantrum, though. Read the instructions. We know this is hard to believe, but when it says, "Jam in tray 3," it's probably not lying.

4. **Look on the bright side.** You'll become so proficient in script copying that you'll always have that Kinko's managerial job to fall back on if times get tough.

5. **Read the scripts.** "What??" Yes, smarty-pants, reading will be key to your development.

6. **Learn to write COVERAGE.** Here's one area in which a college education comes in handy. Coverage is basically a book report, except on a screenplay. Write a two-to-three-page synopsis, then one page (at most) of comments for your boss to read. Address the characterizations, dialogue, structure, and overall marketability.

Make a Wish List

"Goal number 256: Own a Picasso."

THAT'S RIGHT, YOU HEARD US. TURN OFF THE TV, put away the *Enquirer,* and go take a seat at that faux birch desk you bought at Ikea yesterday during an ill-advised spending spree.

"Oh man, do I have to?" Yes! You don't think we are going to let you waste your first few unemployed weeks out of college farting around the roach motel and racking up debt on your parents' credit card, do you? No, it's time to make a wish list of your career goals.

We know, we've already warned you that it's going to be a long haul before you make your dreams come true. Still, that doesn't mean you can sit back and have no dreams.

You see, no matter if you're working in the hallways of a studio or the boardrooms of an I-bank, the next few years of your life are going to be tumultuous. You'll have several jobs, forge a multitude of friendships (and enemy-ships), and question if you're cut out for the Biz every time something bad happens. Distractions will tempt you off course every step of the way, whether they come in the form of dollar signs, fancy titles, or superficial coworkers who convince you to dump your Ford Festiva and mortgage your life for that BMW.

The only way you're going to stay on point is to constantly refer back to the list that you are about to make. It will act as a constant reminder of *why* you chose the Biz in the first place and *what* you wanted to achieve before you become the jaded, bitter, self-loathing individual that you swore you'd never become. (We're going to hold you to this.)

Did you move to L.A. because you always dreamed of being a cinematographer? Or was it because you wanted to tell stories that could positively influence the public's image of our inner cities? Or did you just want to become disgustingly rich with a mansion in the Hills and a Jacuzzi full of supermodels? (Please tell us this one comes after "Find inner peace.")

Regardless of what you decide, please make sure you write it down! Believe us, you'll need this piece of paper in order to keep yourself in check and focused over the long haul that is your career. Otherwise you'll end up achieving all the wrong goals. Like becoming a mean boss, for instance. Laminate this puppy and store it in a safe place. Or, even better, trade lists with your best friend. Make a date to meet in a tropical locale in 20 years to review the lists. A little peer support—and sane competition—will help keep you in check

WISHING ON STARS:
THE GOOD AND THE BAD VERSION

Daniela's Lifetime Goals

1. Make agent by 30.
2. Get writer attached to adapt brother's novel.
3. Start scholarship for young interns.
4. Go to Oscars.
5. Meet De Niro.
6. Friends before funds. Always.
7. Allow myself to bail if I start to become bitter.
8. See name in credits. Feel good about that.
9. Have fun.

Billy's Lifetime Goals

1. House in the hills by 30.
2. Make movie with Will Ferrell
3. Win oscar in honor of mom.
4. Go to Midsummer Night's Dream Lingerie Party at Hef's mansion.
5. Forge relationship with Spielberg. Go on family ski trips together.
6. Marry Keri Russell and don't cheat on her.
7. Write, produce, direct, star in, fund my own movie.

Live for Free or Die Dirt Poor

"$18 for a vodka tonic?!! During Happy Hour?"

LISTEN UP. AS AN INHABITANT OF THIS overconsuming world we live in, your new life is going to be *très cher*. First, there's your rent, likely to hover around $1,000 for a flea-infested bachelor pad in the hood. Then there's the used car, which will guzzle money and gas equally fast, not to mention the high cost of the insurance. Add on clothes, haircuts, a gym membership, and you'll quickly discover that your cost of living is more than your parents' combined income. And finally there's the little issue of entertaining yourself. "I'm sure there's a cheap dive bar on the corner where my drinking habit can thrive," you shrug. Uh, not likely. Dive bar equals hipster bar. A Bud Light will run around eleven bucks.

Thank god for one of the entertainment industry's saving graces: *free liquor.* On any night of any week there are at least a dozen sponsored events where you can not only drink but also eat, dance, and do drugs for no money. Okay, kidding about the drugs. You *do* know to stay away, don't you?

The trick to living large and cheap in Priceywood is to get invited to the right events. Pick up a copy of the local paper (*LA Weekly,* for instance) and scour the ads for free giveaways. Make the city work for you. Special screenings, boutique openings, art gallery showings (red wine in clear plastic cups, booya!) are the norm.

You may have to arrive early to get in, but what do you care? You're unemployed. For the more advanced scrounger, there's the doorman route. Chances are the same few dozen doormen and bouncers will be at the velvet rope each night. Befriend one and you've befriended them all. The best way to do such befriending? A big bill early on. Think of it as an investment that will pay off in the long run. Last, and most difficult, is befriending the **TIK** (Those in the Know). Ideally, this will be Kate Hudson, but since she's unlikely to associate with riffraff like you, start with fellow assistants and FOFs. These are people best hooked into what's hot, what's not, and what's easy to sneak into. (The New Mexico Film Commission's annual "come shoot here" party, for example.) Other events are not so easy to sneak into, such as the *Vanity Fair* Oscar party. Even Madonna has to bring her I.D. to get past those doormen.

FREE AT LAST

Your social life doesn't always have to involve spending lots of money. Here are some good, clean, free ways to have fun:

MUSEUMS:

- **Getty Center** @ 1200 Getty Center Dr.: Free every day.
- **Los Angeles County Museum of Art (LACMA)** @ 5905 Wilshire Blvd.: Second Tuesday of every month is free.
- **MOCA** @ 250 S. Grand Ave.: No-charge musing from 5 P.M. to 8 P.M. on Thursdays.
- **MOCA at the Geffen Contemporary** @ 152 N. Central Ave.: Complimentary viewing of installations on Thursdays from 5 P.M. to 8 P.M.
- **UCLA Hammer Museum** @ 10899 Wilshire Blvd.: Thursdays free.

BEACHES:

- **Dockweiler:** It's O.C. without the 'tude! You can have bonfires, too.
- **El Matador:** Way up the **PCH** (past Zuma), this is one of the most secluded and beautiful beaches. Worth a day trip.
- **Manhattan Beach:** Quintessential southern California with volleyball players and a very clean village (think Disneyland) in which you can shop, eat, and drink. Our happy place.
- **Zuma:** For Malibu locals and big waves.
- **Venice:** For tourists and locals alike, with a crazy cast from which Steinbeck could make his sequel to *Cannery Row*. FYI, the freaks perform on a donation basis only. Go on, give a little.
- **Leo Carillo:** Secluded and gorgeous with tide pools and coastal caves. It's 28 miles north of Santa Monica, and worth every minute of the scenic drive.

LIBRARIES:

Free books and Internet. Besides your local branch, be sure to check out the gorgeous architectural stunner that is the Central Library in Downtown L.A. (630 W. Fifth St.; 213-228-7000; www.lap1.org/central).

AND FOR THOSE ON THE WAGON:

Alcoholics Anonymous, Narcotics Anonymous, and Al-Anon meetings. These are always good for the soul if not just good ol' entertainment. In Hollywood, sobriety is the new addiction. You're likely to spy celebrities here. But please, observe the anonymity rule.

Love Where You Live

"Santa Monica, West Hollywood, Grove adjacent? Or is bohemian chic more me?"

OKAY, SO YOU'VE SET ASIDE YOUR DREAMS, toned down your resume, and got an internship, but your friend Allison is getting really sick of your lazy butt sleeping on her couch. Yes, it's time to start the dreaded apartment search.

If you haven't noticed by now, L.A. is what we like to call sprawling. You probably won't know what neighborhood to settle down in when you first get to town. Your bling-spotting, Chloe-handbag-toting friend assures you the Westside is the Bestside, but it's gonna be a long trek from your paltry $6-a-day internship at NBC . . . so maybe you should just get a cheap little dump in Burbank and call it a day.

Hold on! Location, my friends, will define your life in this mecca o' smog. However, while proximity to your job is paramount, you also don't want to live shacked up with five people in a dump across from a drug den just so you can *walk* to Paramount. When choosing what part of town in which to reside, remember that, like your job, nothing in L.A. is permanent. What's our advice? Find the part of town that best suits your personality.

Next up will be finding the perfect crib. Other than driving around and spying "For Rent" signs (yes, this works, as tedious as it is) and the ubiquitous craigslist, there's L.A.-favorite Westside Rentals (www.west

siderentals.com). We know the fee sucks, but it's worth it. Or split the password with friends. Warning, though: When they say "charming garden" that usually means "patch of weeds with bum living in your parking spot."

Avoid hiring a broker. We know these people are necessary when finding an apartment in New York, but only suckers pay for a broker in L.A. Put that money to good use elsewhere— on a suite at the Beverly Hills Hotel, for example.

YOU ARE WHAT YOU RENT

Here's a little quiz to make sure your splendid tenement will be in the right hood for you:

1. On an average night I am . . .
- **a.** at a dive bar listening to my friend's band.
- **b.** out to dinner with friends and home by 11 P.M. with a hydrating facial mask.
- **c.** watching TV till 4 A.M.
- **d.** sleeping at my one-night-stand's house.

2. The first thing I do when I wake up is . . .
- **a.** jog to spin class!
- **b.** pop two Advil. Okay, sometimes four.
- **c.** pet my cat.
- **d.** scream because I'm already a half hour late for work.

3. Your ideal weekend is spent . . .
- **a.** clubbing, sleeping, shopping, clubbing.
- **b.** watching a movie marathon on my couch.
- **c.** exercising, sunning, and brunching. Then more exercising.
- **d.** making short films, going to museums, smoking.

4. The celebrity I'd most like to bump into at the local coffee shop is . . .
- **a.** Julia Roberts.
- **b.** Chloë Sevigny.
- **c.** Paris Hilton.
- **d.** Sarah Michelle Gellar.

5. Which of the below chain stores are you most likely to frequent?
- **a.** American Apparel
- **b.** J. Crew
- **c.** Urban Outfitters
- **d.** Target

Rate Yourself: Tally up your parts as follows:

1. (a) 2 points; (b) 1; (c) 0; (d) 3 **2.** (a) 1; (b) 2; (c) 0; (d) 3 **3.** (a) 3; (b) 0; (c) 1; (d) 2 **4.** (a) 1; (b) 2; (c) 3; (d) 0 **5.** (a) 2; (b) 1; (c) 3; (d) 0

0–3 points II VALLEY OF THE DOLLS (Burbank, Sherman Oaks, Glendale.)
Why? Because you . . .

- love mini malls, mom-and-pop restaurants, and endless free parking.
- consider a glorious night out to be a dive bar. If it's a really special occasion, you might drive over the hill to Hollywood.
- hate nature. You'd rather be watching Tarantino's latest flick at the Sherman Oaks Galleria.
- can get an apartment at a fraction of the price of the West-side. Who needs the ocean when you have an all-access pass to Universal Studios Citywalk?!

4–5 points II WESTSIDE IS THE BESTSIDE
Why? Because you . . .

- say Namaste is your middle name and sport yoga pants to brunch.
- roam Whole Foods just for fun. You even read the newsletter.
- love the beach, even though you haven't been in seven months.
- swear by Westside offshoots like the Ivy, Fred Segal, and riding your beach cruiser instead of valeting.

6–8 points ‖ EASTSIDE TRUMPS YOUR SIDE

Why? Because you . . .

- are boho chic! In fact, you're so bohemian, you're NOT bohemian.
- cherish Craftsman-style bungalows. No towering apartment complexes for you.
- are an artist. You paint things, build things, and whittle things in your spare time.
- plan to adopt a pit bull.

9 or more ‖ HOLLYWOOD ALL THE WAY

Why? Because you . . .

- love the nightlife, which is now just a stone's throw from your shabby apartment.
- hydrate with martinis, not Vitamin Water.
- dance like nobody's watching and never don the same outfit twice.
- pay less for your rent than that beach bungalow—giving you more disposable cash to throw at bouncers so you'll never have to wait in line again.

Stop Watching *Old School* on Repeat

SO, STILL NO JOB . . . YET. LAST NIGHT WAS FUN, THOUGH, PARTY hopping from one open bar to another. Almost worth the raging hangover. Well, we've got good news. Probably the best news you'll hear all week. This lesson involves embracing your inner couch potato. Yes, we're telling you it is okay to order a greasy pizza, put on your favorite sweats, and get ready to grow fat because today your job is to watch DVDs. Lots and lots and lots of DVDs.

"What the . . . ?"

Hey! This is the *movie* business. In order to do business in this town you have to know movies. And we're not talking about the ones they play on TBS on Saturday (even though we too love *Adventures in Babysitting*). No, we're talking about the classics. The films your parents grew up with. The masterpieces that have inspired everyone from Fellini to Spielberg to Tarantino. The ones that—are you sitting down?—are in black and white.

One of the most common complaints you'll hear in Stupidwood is that kids these days don't know much about movies. Yeah, they watched *Old School* 30 times straight one weekend in college, but ask them who Billy Wilder is and they think you're talking about that

★ *There were films before Will Ferrell. Really.*

water polo player in Sigma Chi. Ask any HPP in Tinseltown and they say the same thing: Nobody watches enough movies. Everyone is too busy trying to discover the next hot writer or break the next It Girl to actually sit down and watch the classics, let alone the shlock they're producing on a daily basis. (Anyone remember *Glitter*?)

You, however, are going to turn yourself into a bona fide movie buff.

- First, start with the American Film Institute's Top 100 Movies. You'll educate yourself in everything Hollywood, as well as fall in love with a slew of new actors. ("That Charlie Chaplin is kinda hot . . .")

- Once you've burned through those (okay, four years later), move on to some foreign directors. Our top ten: Akira Kurosawa, Federico Fellini, Pedro Almodóvar, Ingmar Bergman, François Truffaut, Jean-Pierre Jeunet, Luis Buñuel, Werner Herzog, Andrei Tarkovsky, Jean-Luc Godard.

- Next step: Bone up on funny stuff. Anything by Laurel and Hardy, Harold Lloyd, Woody Allen, Preston Sturges, Billy Wilder, James Brooks, John Hughes, the Coen Brothers, Mel Brooks, Christopher Guest, Monty Python, or any of the greats who crack you up.

- Last up, indy darlings. Get in touch with your artistic side with movies by Jim Jarmusch, Melvin Van Peebles, Jane Campion, David Lynch, Mira Nair, Robert Altman, Hal Hartley, Greg Araki, or Nicole Holofcener.

- Check out our chapter headings. We hand-picked each of these as "must-sees" for young Hollywood hopefuls like you.

- And only when you finish all that can you treat yourself to *Old School* for the 81st time.

CHECK OUT THESE JUICY WEBSITES FOR LISTS OF SOME OF THE BEST FILMS OUT THERE:

IMDb (Internet Movie Database):
www.imdb.com/top_250_film

Time:
www.time.com/time/2005/100movies/the_complete_list.html

American Film Institute:
www.afi.com/tvevents/100years/movies.aspx

Sight and Sound: www.filmsite.org/sightsound.html

Film Four: www.filmsite.org/filmfour.html

AND NOT TO BE FORGOTTEN . . .
MUST-READ BOOKS:

- **What Makes Sammy Run?** by Budd Schulberg. Sammy is the ultimate Hollywood archetype, clawing his way from lowly errand boy to studio chief. And you thought you were ambitious . . .

- **The Last Tycoon,** by F. Scott Fitzgerald. Although unfinished, F. Scott's old yarn about old Hollywood remains relevant. Read it and weep. Literally.

- **The Day of the Locust,** by Nathanael West. Even way back in 1939, when this novel was published, Hollywood's waters were infested with sharks. You'll be struck by how familiar West's characters still seem.

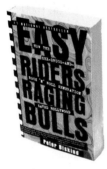

- **Easy Riders, Raging Bulls,** by Peter Biskind. Use these true stories from Hollywood in the '70s to motivate you. Gumption, folks, it's all about gumption.

- **Less Than Zero,** by Bret Easton Ellis. This classic about what it's like to come of age in '80s Hollywood will teach you everything you need to know about your coworkers who were born and raised in L.A. The moral of the story? You probably don't want to raise your kids in this town.

- **The New Biographical Dictionary of Film,** by David Thomson. An idiosyncratic but brilliant assessment of actors, directors, and writers.

- **Acting in Film,** by Michael Caine. Even if you don't want to be an actor (sure ya don't), as an FHPP you should know a little something about the craft. Caine's insights will also prove helpful when you're forced to have a "sit-down" with the lead actress who appears to be sleepwalking through her scenes.

- **Spike, Mike, Slackers, and Dykes: A Guided Tour Across a Decade of American Independent Cinema,** by John Pierson. It's about time you learned about the advent of independent film. And you'll get inspired to make movies that are groundbreaking, not just moneymaking.

Homework Is No Longer a Dirty Word

"I like every Sandra Bullock movie ever made except Miss Congeniality.*"*
"I produced that."
"Oh, I meant Speed 2.*"*
"And that one, too."

YOU'RE IN THE MIDDLE OF A KUROSAWA marathon (up next, *Rashomon!*) when, lo and behold, the phone rings. You've been called in for your first interview! What's the job? Assistant to the junior executive of product placement at some studio that hasn't made a movie in years. Whatever!

Come close now. We need to ask you something. Closer. Have you ever had one of those moments where you stuck your foot so far in your mouth that you started to like the taste? Follow our advice and we promise you'll never have to eat your own foot again. In your career, we mean. Your dating life, not so much. We're not miracle workers here, people. We can only fix one part of you at a time.

You'd be amazed at how many dingbats in this town walk into an interview knowing *absolutely nothing* about the person they're about to meet with. "Listen, Bob, I'm really interested in this opportunity to

come work for your production company." A moment passes, Bob shifting ever so slightly in his Aeron chair.* He clears his throat. "Well, son, I'm glad you're interested in working at a production company. But this here is what we Hollywood types like to call a studio. Those big boxy buildings out there? Those are soundstages. Don't let the door hit your ass on the way out."

We know what you're thinking. How are you supposed to prepare for an interview when all you know is that your friend

The chair that took the office world by storm. When you do get the job, you're not going to want to break your back in a piece of crap $14.99 (with mail-in rebate) Office Depot Naugahyde disaster. Call Human Resources, explain you respect your back and want to play golf when you are 68, if not 88. Whatever you do, get the Aeron, and soon they will all be saying, "How did the new girl get the good chair?"

Roxanne gave your resume to her ex-boyfriend who lives across the hall from this chick who is leaving her job to go teach English in Costa Rica? Well, it's simple. You get Roxanne to give you the ex-boyfriend's keypad combo so you can break into the apartment complex and wait outside the Costa Rica chick's apartment door all night so she can tell you about the job. Seriously? Pretty much. Like we said before, it's a job *hunt*, not a job wait-around-and-see-what-happens.

The dirty truth: You can never do too much research on the person you're about to meet with—and his company. Look up all his credits on **IMDb.com.** Google his career history and who knows, you might find out what personal organizations he belongs to at the same time. (PETA? Good thing you left out that story about last week's hunting trip.) Don't trust the Internet? Then ask everyone you know what they've heard about this bastard. Hollyworld *is* a small world after all.

Pimp Your Personality

YOUR FIRST INTERVIEW IS TOMORROW MORNING, YOU'VE MEMORIZED the company's credits, and now you just need to iron your JCPenney suit—WAIT!! Oh man, thank god we caught that.

We assume you know all the basic rules:

- Show up early.

- Bring extra copies of your resume.

- Don't eat garlic fries during the 24 hours before your appointment.

What you probably don't know is that succeeding in a Hollywood interview is all about The Big P: personality. No one cares if you can speak Portuguese or that you have memorized the direct dials to every executive at every studio. What they do care about is if you're annoying. Or boring. Or unlikable. Having compatible personalities is about the most important part of a successful boss-assistant dynamic, so here are some tips to help you shine:

- **Throw away that suit** and put together a hip-yet-tasteful outfit. Even if you have to borrow a little dough from Dad, it's worth it. No one wants to see your Ann Taylor cream separates disaster from 1993. It's better to show some personal style than look like you want a job at Goldman Sachs.

- **Forget what Sharon at career services said** about having an answer prepared for every question. Instead, practice having a casual conversation (like good acting, it takes work to make it seem spontaneous). Don't list off your top ten favorite screenwriters, but simply drop the names of your favorites where appropriate. Make your future employer feel confident that you're able to hold your own in any setting and won't embarrass them.

- **Mimic them.** You want your potential boss to think you're her mini-me. If the exec says Matt Damon is her favorite actor, say you really admired his work in the *Bourne* series. If she mentions she eats sushi at least six times a week, mention that Hamasaku* has your favorite inside-out spicy tuna roll. Most people in Hollywood have a favorite person of all time, and it's usually themselves.

Hamasaku is an amazing sushi joint with rolls named after regulars like Sarah Michelle Gellar and Christina Aguilera. If you go frequently enough, they might just name a roll after you. Tell owner Toshi we say hi. (11043 Santa Monica Blvd.; 310-479-7636; www.hamasakula.com)

COSTUME DESIGN FOR THE INTERVIEW SCENE

GUYS

Don't . . .

- look like a Brooks Brothers ad. Sporting the suit that you wore to your brother's wedding is bad *unless* you are interviewing at an agency. They're the only ones who dress like bankers.

- overdo the *eau*. Too much cologne will sink you. Rather, don't smell at all.

- sweat. Avoid puddle pits with an undershirt.

- wear anything resembling a paisley.

Do . . .

- be minimal. That is, match some slacks with a pressed button-down without a blazer. Colors should be classic, such as black, navy, or white. Leave the purple polo for the Fourth of July party in Malibu.

- err on the side of a tie. If you're interviewing for an executive at a studio or a member of the older generation, it's better to be safe than sorry. Otherwise, for producers, directors, or writers, go with the fashionable-yet-professional open collar.

- comb your hair. Shaggy belongs with Scooby—on Saturday morning cartoons.

- polish your shoes. Scuff marks read as lazy.

GIRLS

Don't . . .

- roll in all Boho Bum. It may work for fashion stars, but they're millionaires so they can look poor. Transient look *out*, hygiene *in*.

- dress like it's your debut night on *American Idol*. No one wants to see your navel when you bring coffees into the morning staff meeting.

- channel unemployed starlets. Absolutely no hairpieces, handbags with dogs inside, or friends who are your assistants in tow.

- under any circumstances, don a power suit. If that's too much for you to handle, put this book down and go study for the LSAT.

Do . . .

- wear cute, dry-cleaned, and smart-looking designer jeans. Really?? Really. Match them with a freshly starched top and you are simple chic.

- dress up those jeans with cute shoes. If bosses wanted to see your Vans/Levi's combo, they'd roll with you to the Virgin Megastore.

- wear low-cut underwear with low-cut jeans, or risk the receptionist humming "Thong Song" as you exit the office sans job.

- PML it. (Ponytail. Mascara. Lipstick.)

Don't Forget to Say Thank You

"Dear Diary, I had an interview for a job that was just dreamy. I have to get it, Diary. If I don't, I may just die!!!"

SO NOW THAT YOU'VE MASTERED THE ART of the industry interview, it's time to move on to the thank-you letter . . .

Wait! Don't fall asleep!

You can either make or break your chance at a job with this one little piece of paper. Ditch the typed letter and write a handwritten note instead. Whatever industry you are working in, a typed-up letter will come across as too stodgy no matter what you write in it. Besides, you already showed them you could draft a proper letter in your cover letter.

"What about an e-mail? Or a Hallmark e-card?" NO. E-mail's lazy. Which thus leads us to the old-fashioned pen-and-paper number. What's that? You say your handwriting is indecipherable? Call up a friend of the same sex and have him write what you already drafted.

As for the type of card, you want to be careful not to send anything that could turn off your potential employer. No political messages, no strong statements, and definitely nothing cutesy (ducks paddling a dinghy through a lake, geriatrics in purple hats). Black-and-white photos of sailboats, a park scene, a classic painting, a simple pattern . . . Now you're talking.

There's an exception to the rule, however. Sometimes you'll want to find a card that reflects what you know to be your interviewer's interest or passion.

True story: A friend, let's call him Steve, had an interview with a senior agent at ICM who mentioned that she had just got back from a white-water rafting trip in Patagonia. "The best trip of my life. I'd move there someday if I could." The next day Steve was out shopping for a good card to send, when suddenly it hit him like an oar to the head: Steve drove across town to the nearest adventure store and found a card with a photo of a white-water rapid that looked like it might be in Patagonia. He wrote a short and simple "thank you I'd give my left arm to work for you" note and hand delivered it to the ICM receptionist that afternoon. Two hours later Steve gets a call from Human Resources saying he got the job. And let's not forget, all of this happened the day after his interview!

Dear Miss Smith,
It was great meeting you yesterday. Working as your assistant sounds like an amazing experience. Thank you again for considering me.

Best, To the Point Polly

P.S. I've attached a copy of the Harper's article about the pet psychic we discussed. Enjoy!

Dear Joanne,
After our interview yesterday. I feel that I am the perfect candidate for the assistant position. I will work night and day on your behalf. I know both Macintosh and PC. I have studied the great filmmakers. I have committed to memory the names and phone numbers of every major studio executive, agent, and producer in both the Los Angeles and New York areas. I am fully confident that I can fulfill whatever needs you desire.

Let me add this. When I was a little boy with a dream of working in the pictures, I always hoped I would meet someone as talented as you. I truly admire the work you do. Ishtar and Problem Child 2 are films I respect, not only as an aspiring director, but also as a fan of movies. Simply having the chance to work for someone with such amazing taste is an extraordinary opportunity for me. I promise, if you give me this job, I will not let you down.

Sincerely, Overly Effusive Edgar

"I had to get this job. It was the perfect gig for me: A personal assistant to a big-time producer. I could fetch fancy lotions and hair gels by day and work on my writing by night. I wouldn't have to subsist on mac and cheese anymore because it was actually decent pay. The only hitch was that every jobless kid in town was interviewing. How would I set myself apart from the crowd? The day came for my interview. I heard the producer take a call: 'No, make sure they are those *lace* Hanky Pankys. THEY ARE A TYPE OF PANTIES. They can't be sold out, I know

TRUE CONFESSIONS

Neiman's carries them!' There! Perfect. That was it, my big chance. I called my girlfriend who worked at Neiman's and had her fetch me a pair of those lace panties. Fifty dollars was a hefty sum, after the employee discount no less, but it was worth it. I then called my other friend, who was working part-time as a messenger, and had him drop the gift-wrapped panties and a note to my power producer: 'It was a pleasure meeting you. I hope these are the right color.' I had the job before dinner."

—A.Q.

Find a Mentor

"You're hired. But first, please sign your soul over to us on the dotted line."

HOW EXCITING! YOU'VE MASTERED OUR RULES of interviewing so well that you've gotten not one but *two* job offers. Way to go. Now comes the tough part. You've made a pro and con list, you've chewed your fingernails down to the nub, and you've talked it over with every sucker who walked into your favorite coffee shop yesterday. "Golly, so this is how Meryl Streep felt." Let's review.

Behind Door #1: The widely coveted executive assistant position at a world-renowned movie studio. You heard they interviewed 50 people for this one, including Madonna's longest-lasting assistant. And guess what? They chose you! Boy oh boy. The pay is higher than most jobs, the potential for making contacts is infinite, and the perks are awesome (did someone say expense account?!). Talk about Caviar Dreams! You feel like you've won the lottery. . . Not so fast.

Behind Door #2: Your typical entry-level position at an independent production company. Two bosses, the overtime is capped at a laughable five hours a week, and the only perk you'll get is first dibs on the staff lunch left-overs. (Yes, your salary will dictate that you eat leftovers or starve.) However, the job isn't all bad. You'll get to read scripts *and* give your opinion on them. Your boss will need to rely on your decision-making skills to either pass or consider a project. You talked to the last assistant, and he was actually in meetings. And not just when the lowly creative executive had food poisoning. The end result? You'll actually be learning.

This is a no-brainer. Hands down, go with Door #2. You see, the one thing this industry lacks more than any-thing else—well, besides intelligence,

Who . . .	Lives in . . .
Studio Exec Erika	Brentwood (currently adding third wing)
Producer Pat	Santa Monica
Agent Angela	Beverly Hills
Director Dirk	The Hills
Screenwriter Sara	Venice

modesty, a conscience . . . sorry, we digress—is **Mentors.** That's right. Mentors are the bosses who will look at you as *more than* a professional slave. In fact, they will see you for who you are—a living, breathing, thinking individual with the potential to grow in this job. A mentor-boss will take time out of his busy day to explain something you don't understand and trust you to take on responsibilities that you actually might not be cut out for. Hell, he might even steal one of your ideas for his own advancement. Doesn't it sound great?

The greedy fool who took the job behind Door #1 became little more than a phone answerer, scheduler, and sometimes dog pooper-scooper. No one ever asked for her opinion, only for coffee. "Two packets of Splenda this time, Clark." "My name is Candace." "What does that have to do with anything?"

Always choose the mentor. Your long-term prospects are more important than your short-term purchases.

THE ASPIRE CHART
(AKA WHICH HPP DO YOU WANT TO BE?)

Your mentor should be someone you want to emulate. For example, do you fantasize about having as hectic a schedule as Angela? Or is Dirk's party life the one you want? Ed's lavish mansion in B'wood? Check out this personality chart to see whose life you're best suited for:

Shoes . . .	Spends nights . . .	Dreams of . . .	On bedside table . . .
Prada	Green-lighting	Opening a B&B in Napa	Her own autobiography (unfinished)
Nike Cross Trainers, for comfort	Going over latest budget overages	Getting studio to green-light movie about Aristotle	Historical biography of Chairman Mao
Jimmy. Just Jimmy.	Drinking with clients at the Four Seasons	Poaching Johnny Depp from UTA	Advil
Same black sneaks since '85	Watching Polanski movies with friends in screening room	Signing Scarlett to next movie, then bedding her	Tom Ford photo collection
Crocs, if not barefoot	Procrastinating by watching old *Golden Girls* episodes	Writing a novel	Anything by Barbara Kingsolver

Know Who's Who

"Are we still holding? Hang up. I don't hold for that loser."

IT'S DO OR DIE TIME, BABY! THE FINAL crunch. Because just like that day sophomore year after you skipped your econ seminar all semester and found out there was a midterm the next day, it's time to start cramming.

Tomorrow you start the big job. But you know nothing. Even though in your interview you said you knew, and we quote, "everything." That included every partner at every agency, every exec at every studio, and every piece of information that was ever printed in **the trades.**

"Um, what's the trades?" Oh man, like only the most widely read periodicals in Hollywood. (*Variety* and *Hollywood Reporter.* You should have already gotten your subscription. Like months ago. And don't just look at the pictures.)

★ *Required reading. Daily. No excuses.*

The most important thing to know before you start the big J-O-B? Who is who. Yes, you're going to need to quickly learn who are the big fish, who are the small fish, and who are the small fish who think they are big fish. And, you better know what kind of fish you are working for. Your boss's place in the hierarchy will determine (1) how you should answer the phone, (2) what attitude to take with people, and (3) if you need to quickly start looking for a job with someone better (i.e., you are working for, not one, but three junior agents at Gersh).

Some very fundamental questions to ask yourself about your new boss:

■ Is he or she a seller or a buyer?

■ An exec at a studio, or running a production company?

■ A big-time agent, or no-time agent? If Big-Time Agent calls about your small-time project, you better know who he/she is and find your boss. "Why didn't you tell me Lorenzo called?!" is code for, "You idiot, now we'll never get Kirsten that part!!"

THE BASICS (JUST IN CASE YOU'RE NOT CLEAR):

- **AGENCIES (sellers):** Agents represent all the important people: actors, directors, writers, producers. Pushy, persistent, and petulant, they try to procure jobs for their clients, negotiate their contracts, and take a 10 percent commission for doing so. The good? Rep Will Smith and you are powerful. The bad? You are at the constant beck and call of some very demanding personalities.

- **MANAGERS (sellers):** Managers also represent the talent, getting anywhere from 10 to 15 percent commission, but usually have a smaller list of clients and deal with more day-to-day problems (how to score their B-list client a ticket to the new David Fincher premiere, for example). The good? They are often the ones responsible for guiding a client to an all-star career (Renée Zellweger even took her manager when she won the Oscar) and, when they play a role in developing a client's project, they can (unlike agents) sometimes finagle themselves a producer credit. The bad? Managing is like parenting. Lots of dirty diapers.

- **STUDIOS (buyers):** Studios decide what movies to make and give the producers, writers, actors, and directors lots of money to go do so. The good? Only a studio can green-light a movie. The bad? No matter how much *creative* power studios think they have, they're pretty much just banks.

- **PRODUCERS (buyers *and* sellers!):** Perpetually stuck in the middle, the producers have to convince financiers to fork over money for their pictures (this can be from a studio, an independent investment group, or some rich dude in Texas), as well as convince the talent to make, rewrite, or star in these movies. The good? Whether in a story meeting in the office or talking to the director on set, producers actually get to manipulate how a movie turns out. The bad? How much power can you truly wield when you've given it all to an egomaniacal director?

- **THE REST OF 'EM (not able to buy or sell):** These people were nominated for an Oscar in 1932 and still won't let the dream die. If they call, don't be rude. Everybody is a somebody. Even if that was a long, long time ago. You're making dreams for a living, people—not killing them.

There Is No Silver Platter

OH, THE GLITZ, THE GLAMOUR. DO YOU KNOW THAT DURING OUR first week on the job we went to two premieres, danced at four clubs, mingled with celebs galore, and were both offered raises? You didn't know that? Oh, that's right, because THIS NEVER HAPPENED.

What was our first week on the job really like? A whole bunch of crap, really. Long hours, dinner after dinner at our desks, and a drunken, best-if-forgotten night at some dive bar in Culver City. Once again, we experienced a case of the underwhelming Hollywood experience. Get ready for a whole lot of 'em.

We know, we're killing your buzz, but before you get too excited about what lies ahead, we want to remind you that what you are about to go through is more like a war than a dream. No matter what they say, the road to Hollywood power is paved with blood, sweat, and assistants' tears. For every inspiring story about the guy from Southie who sold a script to Harvey Weinstein there are 3,000 more about the people who couldn't get anyone to return their calls. And even Southie himself blew that opportunity.* Oh, stop that crying. We're not here to tell you that you won't make it. We're here to tell you to be realistic.

The truth? You're going to be an assistant longer than you'd like. You will grow sick of this first job (and possibly the second). You probably won't be rolling with Justin Timberlake and crew at his Hollywood mansion in the near future. And the closest you'll get to a house in the 'Bu (Malibu, you neophytes) is the ten-foot sliver of public beach littered with trash. The important thing is patience. Perseverance is key. Pick yourself up and try again. THERE IS NO SILVER PLATTER, PEOPLE! Wow, we really know how to hammer a point home, don't we?

Well, there's a reason for that. Namely, all the people who came before you. Just read the following true accounts (or horror stories, if you will) of some folks who learned this lesson the hard way. Luckily, they lived to tell the tale.

See the 2003 documentary Overnight *for a true-life cautionary tale about Troy Duffy, a writer-director* (Boondock Saints) *who went from A-list to no-list in a matter of months. The moral of the story? Don't look a gift horse in the mouth.*

E! TRUE LIFE HOLLYWOOD STORIES:
FRESH OFF THE BUS

"It was my first night in La La Land. Friends I knew from college planned a huge party in their apartment—so I could experience the real Hollywood, they said. I pulled out the new tube top and straightened my hair. I was out here to meet people, so why not start immediately, right? Wrong! Not only did some guy with bad breath trap me in the corner the entire night, but I think he spiked my drink with Metamucil. I spent the next two days holed up in my friend's bathroom. To this day I still don't go to house parties." **—Sally W.**

"I'd taken a flight here from Tennessee and met the nicest girl on the plane. We both happened to be reading *Leaves of Grass*. When we landed, we exchanged numbers. 'Call me!' she smiled, toting her pink roller bag out the door. So I did. No call back. She must have deleted my message by accident, I thought. So I called again. And again. And again. Like Jon Favreau in *Swingers*. So whatever, I get over it. Until I see her out at a bar a few weeks later. 'Yo, Casey,' I say. 'Remember me? Whitman fan, we shared a pitcher at the St. Louis airport TGIF?' Just a blank stare. She was playing dumb blonde. And that's when I realized. Girls in L.A. suck. Outside of L.A., sure, they'll practically take you to meet their mom and dad after the first date. But in Hollywood? I learned quickly that I'd have to look somewhere else for that wife. Which, by the way, I still haven't found." **—Jordan H.**

"I already had a job when I moved out here. It was my first day and an assistant offered me her boss's tickets to a Dodger game. But then came the catch. I had to drive the boss to the airport first. And pick up his daughter from middle school (in the Valley no less). And take care of his three dachshunds for the weekend, who, by the way, had to be walked every hour so as to avoid bladder infections. It was after that weekend that I realized, giveaways are never given. They're traded. Most likely for your soul. My advice? Avoid dogs with bad bladder control." **—Kevin T.**

"I had just moved to L.A. and was desperate for a new wardrobe. So I went where every girl goes when she comes here for the first time. Kitson. It was a dream come true. I was shopping at the same place as Eva Longoria and Lindsay Lohan. So I shopped and I shopped and I shopped. I didn't even look at the price tags. This was my treat. And I'd saved up all that money working at BCBG last summer. Well, let me just say this. My credit limit still hasn't recovered from that day. In fact, I haven't been shopping since. Do you know what that will do to a girl's spirit in this city? Yeah, it's crushing. Like mope-around-the-apartment-eating-Pringles-and-watching-reruns-of-*90210* crushing. I can't even fit into those jeans now. The lesson? Kitson is for celebutantes, not 22-year-olds without a job." **—Jessica I.**

Congratulations. You've completed phase 1 of your HPP training. Before you proceed to phase 2 however, here's another quiz to see if you've retained anything. If you fail, may we refer you back to the How to Tell If You're a Moron quiz (p. 4). (P.S. You've got four more tests to get through before you're done. Stop your crying already.)

THE TINSELTOWN TEST: TAKE 1

1. **You're new to town, brunching on the $2 egg platter at Denny's, and this guy at the table next to you claims that he's a producer and wants to take you out for coffee. You . . .**
   a. think he's hitting on you and tell him to screw off.
   b. pretend that you're deaf and can't understand what he's saying.
   c. agree to go across the street and grab a coffee with him.
   d. go into the bathroom for a quickie.

2. **You're at your first Hollywood interview. It's an entry-level job at a tiny production company known for movies starring Tori Spelling. Which of the below facts about yourself *should* you mention to your potential employer:**
   a. You've watched *Casablanca* 33 times.
   b. You grew up answering the phones at your father's plastic bag factory.
   c. You have a 4.0 GPA.
   d. You think Tori Spelling is underrated as an actress.

3. **You've been in L.A. for a month and still don't have a job. You should spend your free time . . .**
   a. lounging on the Ikea couch, eating Ding Dongs, and watching Netflix.
   b. interning at the video dubbing lab for free.
   c. daydreaming about all the amazing accomplishments you're going to achieve when you're president of the studio.
   d. All of the above.
   e. None of the above.

4. **You just had an amazing interview with the heads of UTA. You . . .**
   a. send an e-card.
   b. send a typed letter thanking them for the opportunity.
   c. handwrite a note thanking them for the opportunity.
   d. do nothing and wait for them to call.

5. **You have several job offers. You decide to pick the one which . . .**
   a. lets you learn.
   b. pays the most.
   c. deals with the most powerful people.
   d. sounds the best when you're out at Hyde.

ANSWERS: 1. c; **2.** b; **3.** d; **4.** c; **5.** a

TAKE 2: PRE-PRODUCTION

OKAY, TROOPS! LISTEN UP HERE. THIS HERE IS WHEN WE LEAVE the safe and cushy nest of Development and move into PRE-PRODUCTION, aka Assistant Boot Camp.

Under our expert tutelage, you will now learn to conquer the world of answering phones, scheduling meetings, booking travel, organizing files, and pretty much hating life.

"But the phones scare me!"

"I can't fit three meetings into sixty minutes!!"

"I was hired as the Christmas coordinator. What does that mean??"

"I think I need to go home to Tallahassee. This whole assistant thing sounds scary . . ."

Hey! Hold up there, Tally. You're going nowhere. No way. In Boot Camp, quitting is not a word. Neither is "special treatment," for that matter. Yeah, that includes you, too, fancy Princeton boy. From here on out there'll be no crying, whining, arguing, back talking, or fist fighting. You'll do what we say, and like it too. You hear us now?? You sorry, good-for-nothing, sad sacks of wannabe power players . . .

"Sir, yes sir!"

Onward, soldiers.

BRAND YOUR BOSS: WHICH GENRE DO YOU HAVE?

Whether you work for a partner at an ad agency, a congressman on the Hill, or a director on the lot, your boss can be classified by a movie genre. So before we move on to our next lesson, we thought this would be a good time to discuss the different types of bosses and what kind of movie you are working in.

Use the handy descriptions below to prepare yourself to (1) identify your boss and (2) learn to cope. And yes, some bosses have been known to exhibit more than one personality type. Don't worry; you can handle it. We hope.

HORROR SHOW BOSS

"Forget my wife's birthday again and I'll shove that headset so far up your—"

The Horror Show is the most infamous Hollywood boss, the one most often depicted in pop culture (see Ari Gold on *Entourage* or Kevin Spacey in *Swimming with Sharks*). He screams, he yells, he throws things. However, there is something to be said for having a boss who "acts out." You see, chances are that ten minutes after he has gotten his aggression out (e.g., taken his 9-iron to your keyboard), he'll forget why he was mad in the first place. Our advice: Never take things personally. Instead, let the insults bounce right off your thick skin and move on to what's important—your work. After all, it's all the Horror Show really cares about.

ACTION BOSS

"Are you done yet?"
An Action Boss demands *movement* at all times. That means if she's asked you to send out a script an hour ago, she expects the producer to already have it on his desk. Hence, you must never dillydally, instead completing tasks right away and immediately reporting back that you have done so. Yes, you're going to be exhausted by the end of the day, but at least you won't have to dodge staplers. And this go-go-go mentality will help you in the future when you realize that, deep down, everyone in the Biz wants things done "five minutes ago."

ROMANTIC COMEDY BOSS

"Can you do me this one favor, sweetie?"
Oh, you're going to feel so lucky the first few weeks working with the Rom Com. This boss, as charming as they come, tells the best jokes, invites you in on pitch meetings, and even remembers your birthday! "I'm in love!" you'll tell yourself. Beware, though. After a few weeks of the warm-and-fuzzies you're going to realize there's a big downside. He'll feel so good about treating you so well that he'll also feel entitled to ask you to do things *not* in your job description. We're talking babysitting the kids, picking up the dry cleaning, and planning Uncle Marty's 80th birthday party. How to deal? Don't get sucked in. That means not accepting every one of the free lunch offers or extra premiere tickets. We promise, the fewer freebies you accept the more you'll feel empowered to say no when it counts. Did you really need to go to that early screening of *Christmas with the Kranks: The Grandparent Years*? Show some self-control, already.

DRAMA BOSS

"WHERE are my pink Post-its?? Good god, don't tell me we are OUT of pink Post-its!"
Oh, no, you've got the Drama Queen. This means that your days are going to be filled with nonstop stress, urgent deadlines, and bomb scares. You see, the Drama Queen doesn't get "the joke." She thinks her job's about curing cancer, not making fluffy popcorn movies. There's no sense of humor here, and you're going to go to bed each night feeling like you might die unless you make your boss happy. Guess what? You won't. Working in the Biz is *never* life or death, so you must remain levelheaded at all times, even when she's running down the halls screaming, "We're all going to lose our jobs unless I get ten copies of this directors list right now!" In order to appease the Drama Queen you must do the following: Outwardly appear to care about your job, but inwardly tell yourself, "Chill. The only one who's going to lose her job is you, Boss, and that's only because you're a super-duper freak."

COMEDY BOSS

"Psst. Do you know who this chick Helen Mirren is? Is she that tween from Nickelodeon?"

Your boss is so funny. That is, so *bad at his job* that he's funny. You can't believe he got this far in his career! So you laugh, and then you cry, and then you laugh and cry some more. You're terrified that you got stuck working for an idiot and, as a result, will be perceived as an idiot by association. Don't fret, because there's something great about working for total morons: You get to outsmart them. For every mediocre move they make, you are there to pick up the pieces *and* let everyone know it was you who thought to change that action role from male to female—which in turn got Jodie Foster attached—not them.

THRILLER BOSS

"Get me Kevin! No, call Marcy first. Scratch that, make it Les. WAIT! No, Theresa, I MEAN TOM . . ."

One of the most difficult types of bosses, the Thriller has more personalities than Oprah has dollars. One moment the Thriller can be all lovey-dovey, bringing you Mocha Frappuccinos just "to say thanks," and the next criticizing you for not ordering the right shade of yellow legal pad. What do you do? Ride the roller coaster. While the Thriller may be up and down emotionally, not to mention her feelings about *you,* it's best to go with the flow. If she loves you one hour, bask in the glory. If she hates you the next, put your head down, do your work, and make sure to order the right shade of paper next time. And even if you feel like you might check into the crazy house at any minute, you'll at least *seem* like the stable one.

FAMILY BOSS

"I love my assistant. Really, we're more than just colleagues. We're friends. I don't know what I'd do without her."

Yeah, right! She also claimed she was going to treat you to a massage and share half her bonus with you too, right? You are too gullible. You see, the Family Boss DOES NOT EXIST. No such thing. No matter how nice or generous or supportive your boss may seem, you will never be BFFs. (No, she will not be a bridesmaid at your wedding, even though she pretends to care about your pending nuptials.) So just accept the fact that no boss is perfect. And if you find someone who says his or her boss is, run. This person is a liar.

Thicken Up That Skin

"Sweetie, will you be a doll and freshen up my coffee? Just a spritz of bourbon this time."

SWEETIE. HONEY. DEAR. SKANK!! YOU WILL BE called a lot of names in this job. Some patronizing, some mean, some so downright offensive that a call to H.R. would not be unwarranted. But you'd never do that. Why not? Because your wise elders here are telling you that being insulted is just another rite of passage in whatever business you choose to work in. Especially in Hollywood, where name-calling is an art form. There are even certain notorious HPPs who've built their entire reputation on their ability to dream up insults for their assistants.

"This is so demeaning," you'll think to yourself after enduring your first verbal assault. "I haven't been called this many names since Vickie Hammers thought I slept with her boyfriend sophomore year."

Are your feelings a little hurt? Well, too bad. Because the sooner you stop crying that river the sooner you'll grow the thick skin you're going to need to survive. "How do I do that?" Simple. The key to not getting your feelings hurt is to understand the psychological principle of projection at work here. That's right, nine times out of ten, when your boss is cruel to you, it's only because he is feeling bad about himself. What better way to lift his own spirits than by bringing yours down? Now that you see what's really going on, don't you feel better? We thought so.

Case in point: You may hate it when that agent from Endeavor thinks you'll be more likely to have your boss return the call if he calls you "babe" over the phone, but it's really not worth getting your panties in a bunch. Why? He could be the same guy who recommends you for that C.E. job at Scott Free (Ridley and Tony Scott's company, but you know that already). As they say, sticks and stones will break your bones . . . well, you went to third grade. The exception? Slut. No one is ever allowed to call you a slut.

Being Awake Means Being at Work

"9-t0-5??
HAHAHAHAHA
HAHAHA!"

YOU HEAR THAT? THAT'S THE SOUND OF US laughing. The last time we experienced an 8-hour day is that time from college when we drank a whole bottle of Cuervo and slept 16 hours straight. We know, the long hours in Hollywood don't make much sense. We're not in The Biz of Saving Lives, after all. Yet, somehow, Hollywood-types manage to work all day, every day. Everyone feels a little more important that way. That means 12-hour days. If you're lucky.

Agencies are the most notorious for their long hours. Rise and shine at 5 A.M. to get to the Bagel Broker by 5:45 to pick up the pastries for the morning staff meeting. Before you know it, it's 11 P.M. and you're still driving in circles around Laurel Canyon trying to find the house of the actor who desperately needs the TV pilot now sitting in your passenger seat. We know, it makes you want to drive your car over that cliff with the Hollywood Sign. Don't. Because peace and quiet are just around the corner . . . when you retire at Leisure Village in 50 years.

As a rule, underlings shall always be available for the boss. This means you'll need to be reachable on your way to the dentist, at the dentist, during the triple root canal, and after the painkillers kick in at midnight. Even if all that happens on a Saturday. You see, you never know when business is going to pop up, so if you go to the movies, church, or even a funeral, reserve a seat by the door, put your phone on vibrate, and wait to be called at the most inopportune time.

Our advice to get through the day: (1) caffeine, (2) sugar, (3) an I.V. of Red Bull. This is what we like to call the triple whammy of joy. (Note: See WARNING!)

Seriously, though—if you must go out, don't go *ALL* out. Limit yourself to two drinks on a school night. If you have to go to that coworker's party at Sky Bar, leave at midnight, not 2 A.M. When at home, sleep, don't catch up on your TiVo, even though those episodes of *South Park* are looking pretty tempting about now.

As for working on the weekends? Here's a tip that has saved our hides time and time again: Never ever, under any circumstances (we-will-find-you-and-hunt-you-down-if-you-disobey-our-orders) should you answer your cell phone on the weekend.

"Are you serious? I'll end up dead or, worse, fired!" Oh, stop crying, you big baby. All we're saying is that you should simply let the call go to voicemail. That way you'll have time to figure out how to (1) do it, or (2) fabricate an excuse of why it can't be done, or (3) delegate it to someone else. Once you've solved the problem?? Party. Dance. Rage. Carpe that diem, baby, because you only live once. Besides, you'll need some stories for the grandkids other than "I spent my twenties answering phones and copying scripts."

WARNING!
HOW NOT TO SURVIVE THE 12-HOUR DAY

Per our all-time favorite *Saved by the Bell* episode . . .
We're sure you remember it. And if you don't, then we probably shouldn't be talking to you in the first place. Really, it's actually pretty amazing how often this episode of *Saved by the Bell* comes up in our life (we're guessing at least once a month). Not to know what we're talking about is pretty much a generational sin. Like not knowing the steps to "The Macarena" or the words to "Hit Me Baby One More Time."

Yes, we're talking about the Jesse-Spanno-Gets-Addicted-to-Caffeine-Pills-and-Sings-I'm-So-Excited-Right-Before-She-Has-a-Mental-Breakdown Episode.

★ Showgirls–*scaring kids straight since '95.*

"Oh! Of course I remember that. It's the stuff of legends."

There ya go! I mean, is it any wonder Elizabeth Berkley beat out thousands for that part in *Showgirls*?

But we digress. The moral of this story is that you should NEVER, EVER resort to using controlled substances to get through the long workday. Trust us, it will start off as a few double espressos after lunch, then on to half a bottle of No-Doz per day, followed by the hard stuff, and ending with, yup, the Betty Ford Center.

For those feeling nostalgic, you can usually find the clip we're talking about with a quick Google search.

Become Psychic

"Get me the guy who did that research on that place I want to go, can I see the production reports from yesterday, why hasn't my new computer come, I'm out of those paper clips I like, and hellooooo, can I have that iced tea I asked for two minutes ago? It's like I'm the only one working around here. Seriously."

HEY, YOU. YES, YOU OVER THERE! STOP LIS-tening to your iPod and start paying attention to what you're reading. Yes, we promise it'll be worth it—especially this sage tip. If you don't, you're not going to get past Day Uno on the job. There, we knew that'd get your attention. Now listen closely . . .

Ask any boss in any industry and they'll tell you that the thing they appreciate most in an assistant is the ability to anticipate. "Anticipate what?" Well, everything, really. That includes who they'll want to call in an hour, what file they'll need for their 3 P.M. videoconference, the new biodegradable yoga mat they need for their 8 P.M. flow class, and which narcotic they'll choose to abuse later tonight . . . Okay, so we kid. A little bit.

The god's honest? Your new boss is going to be a busy person. Always. At any given moment she will be juggling 45 different thoughts, and only half of those will be how much she hates you. Regardless, it is precisely because of the insane pace of this business that your mind will now need to act purely as an extension of your boss's. Forget being your own person who sees life in your very own unique way. From this moment on you will live and breathe inside the boss's brain. So what if it happens to be damaged beyond all recognition! That's just another reason to stay away from the club scene (more on this later).

Example: If your boss the Agent is figuring out how to cast her unhappy actor client in the new Michael Mann movie, she's not going to have time to tell you to get his demo reel ready for the 5 P.M. FedEx shipment. No, you should have had the label printed yesterday when you first heard the client was interested in the project. Another: Let's say you heard the company is ordering sushi for the staff lunch. The problem? Your boss had it for dinner last night. Hence, you better have an alternative lunch option sitting in front of him by the time the meeting starts. We suggest the famous McCarthy salad from the Polo Lounge. No mercury overdoses will go down on your watch!

We know, you're thinking this seems rather crazy. "You want me to read my boss's mind?? I came to Hollywood to be Louis B. Mayer, not

Miss Cleo." Well, sorry, Louis, but it's this way or the highway. Bosses don't have time to handhold their assistants, so you're going to need to be self-sufficient if you're going to support their needs. If you can't, then they might as well save the few thousand bucks they pay you and blow it on shoes (or strippers or blackjack or Botox or . . . whatever vice your boss has fallen victim to).

PROJECT M.A.S.S. (MULTITASKING AMIDST THE SHIT STORM):

Along with anticipation, multitasking is a key component of an assistant's success. Here's a test to figure out whether you need to brush up on your skills:

1. If I yell out nine names in a row, can you call them all in sequential order during your boss's 45-second bathroom break that also doubles as call-return-time? Wait, did you really just think about your answer? Oy. Time-outs for thinking, young pup, are not allowed. (Score: zero.)

2. "Box-office chart, July's credit card statement, notes on the Aztec project, file on that sexual harassment suit, and Monday's newspaper with the article on the competitors . . ." You: rank these in order of importance. Ha, trick question! They're all *equally* important, silly. Meaning, they all better be on your boss's desk already or else you're canned. (Score: negative zero.)

3. The waiting area is jammed with a dozen **HI MAPs** (High Maintenance Peeps). They want eight espressos, three diet cream sodas, and a calcium-enriched water. Can you grab all of these while yelling what movies opened last weekend and flirting with the agent who can help you get that job at John Well's company? You think so? Man, you better know so or the first impression you leave will be as "that slow girl who doesn't even read the trades." And get me a highlighter. Purple. (Score: Ugh, we can't even say it.)

4. "Book the corner table with Sam Shepard at Barney Greengrass and tell Michael Hiller to have my Arnold Palmer lukewarm by the time I get there." If you're even trying to figure out which of these are actual real living people and which are not, then stop. Please, just stop. You've failed.

Oh, stop that crying. We're not saying you're out of the game, just to pick up the pace or be demoted to minor leagues (the Accounting Department, FYI).

P.S. If you're wondering, here's the answer to number 4: Sam is an actor/writer who is married to Jessica Lange. Barney Greengrass is the restaurant on the top floor of the Barneys store in Beverly Hills. Michael Hiller is the name of a waiter we made up. And an Arnold Palmer is a half iced tea, half lemonade. You better remember all that. You will be tested.

Love Your Cubicle

SEE THAT CUBE? YES, THE ONE WITH THE BROKEN CHAIR, dinosaur of a computer, and '80s-inspired panel siding. You are going to be spending the next 8,760 hours in this shithole. No, that does not include sleeping.

It's a law of the universe that the minute you leave your desk, the proverbial shit will hit the fan. Unfortunately for you, and your bladder, that leaves only one solution: You. Don't. Leave.

The first rule of Assistant Club: *Leaving your desk is a no-no*. The second rule of Assistant Club: This includes hospitalizations, deaths in the family, and bathroom breaks. Assistant returning from the restroom to find his voicemail light on: "Sorry, boss, nature called." "Well, you know what? The head of CAA called and that's way more important. You're fired."

Hence, we've devised the following pick-me-ups to make the most of your new cave, ahem, we mean home.

- **The Beautification Project.** You might think it impossible, but there is a way to make your new space pretty. Whether that means bringing in family photos or installing aluminum siding from Home Depot, you must take pride in your new space. This isn't college any more; dormitory drudgery is no longer in vogue. Step it up!

- **Prepare for Nuclear Disaster.** Like a sailor on a submarine, you are going to need to stock up on all your favorite things. We recommend provisions to sustain you for at least three to four months of nonstop busy work. Candy, chamomile tea, dental floss, hand moisturizers . . .

- **Mi Casa Es Su Casa.** Like they say, if you can't go to the party, bring the party to you. Bribe colleagues over with some mini Snickers or, even better, a swig of whiskey from your flask. How are you supposed to do this when any colleague you could possibly lure over is also chained to a desk? Oh, don't you get it? By getting other assistants to leave their desks you are increasing their chances of getting fired, and yours of being promoted. Suckers.

- **Aerobics Class.** Beware. After two weeks of sitting at your desk you're liable to develop a condition that will henceforth be referred to as Growing Ass. The human body is not meant to sit for 12 hours a day while consuming nothing but stale Sun Chips and Sprite. Hence, desk aerobics are essential to warding off lard. Jumping jacks, downward dogs, and tricep lifts off the side of your chair are all acceptable.

CUBICLE NO-NOS:

No matter what, please don't fill your cube with the following:

- **Pictures of your cats.** Fine, be a cat lady, but please don't subject us to your sad life.
- **Soft porn.** Jessica Biel sure looks hot in that bikini. Too bad you got fired, perv.
- **Perishables.** Candy is okay. Celery sticks are not. Your desk is not a fridge.
- **Religious idols.** Separation of church and state!
- **Inspirational quotes.** This ain't Oprah. Sure, they worked for your high school English teacher, but cheesy mottos do nothing but make us hate you.

"My Thunderbird was my baby. Like even if I lost all my friends and went homeless I'd be okay because I still had my 1966 candy-apple-red T-bird. Which goes to explain why I went ballistic when the guard at the gate called to say a Hummer had run into it. My boss was in a meeting so I ran down to look at the damage. I was speechless. My baby was now a junkyard dog. Even if I managed to replace the hood, there was still the problem of the whole smashed engine thing. I wanted to lie down and have that Hummer run over me, too. Or at least take a baseball bat to its windshield. When I got back to my desk, my boss was sitting there reading something off my computer screen. I knew right away. It was the screenplay I had been writing during my free time at work. 'Am I Bruce?' he asked me. I gulped. You see, it was a slasher pic that was really a metaphor for all my time in Hollywood. Bruce was the killer who could make people bleed to death with just one look and, well, my boss recognized himself in the character. I tried to deny it, even coming up with some story about how it was based on my stepfather, but my boss didn't care. Not only was I fired, but Bruce would never make it to the big screen. Yeah, I guess my employee contract said that whatever I created during work hours or on the company computer was property of the company. Two things: Never leave your desk and, if you must, close out all your windows." **—P.O.**

TRUE CONFESSIONS

Be the Phone

"Your agent's on line 1, your mother's on line 2, your therapist's on line 3, and someone named Candy from Crazy Girls is on 4."

WE KNOW, THE PHONES SCARE YOU. ALL THOSE blinking lights, all that weird terminology, the boss screaming obscenities at you . . . Get used to it. Everything in this business—from making deals, to green-lighting movies, to convincing Keira Knightley to do that horror flick—can and will take place over the phone. In fact, the phones are such an important part of your job that we're dedicating more than one lesson to them (see "The Conversation," "Don't Say a Word," and "When a Stranger Calls" for more).

From now on it's your goal to eat, drink, and sleep the phones. It's your job to block the crazies from getting through and to push that urgent call to the top of the list. You will also now be your boss's actual right hand. His ability to dial the phone, let alone endure the length of time it takes for someone to pick up, no longer exists. You will pretty much waste away the best years of your youth dialing, connecting, conferencing, muting, and holding. Let's not even start on how you're supposed to do the other parts of your job—scheduling, travel arrangements, research on the Knights Templar—at the same time. It won't be long before your personal cell will ring at 2 P.M. on a Sunday and you'll answer "Bobby Schleggerhoffer's office!" out of habit. (Don't worry, your mom will eventually get used to this.)

How do you keep track of the 300 incoming calls coming your way every day? It's a wonderful little invention called the **phone sheet.** Learn it, live it, love it. This database will become both your best friend and best resource, allowing you to catalog who's incoming, who's outgoing, who's need-to-call, and who's never-in-your-life-do-you-call-back.

HERE ARE SOME TERMS YOU WILL NOW LEARN AND NEVER, EVER FORGET:

- **Left Word:** To have left a message. "Where's Reese?!" Boss yells. "I left word for her precisely 3 hours, 22 minutes, and 7 seconds ago," you respond cheerfully.

- **Rolling:** The act of calling one person after another after another. "Let's start rolling calls, jackass! My phone sheet is running about two miles long."

- **Need to Call:** The person your boss feels the need to call *later*. "Make Bruckheimer a Need to Call. I need to ask him to cut that helicopter inferno sequence out of the movie."
- **Dropped Call:** The caller you *forgot* to add to the phone sheet. Important!! The dropped call is something to avoid at all costs! Trust us, your heart will sink to depths you didn't know existed when you wake up in the middle of the night in a cold sweat thinking, "Holy shit, Jeffrey Katzenberg called two days ago and I totally forgot to add him to the phone sheet." When your boss finds out? You better hope the manager at Fatburger has forgiven you for quitting the minute you found out that you got this great job . . . from which you have just been fired.

SIZE MATTERS:
WHOSE PHONE SHEET IS LONGER?

One easy way to discern a person's rank in Tinseltown would be a brief glance at his phone sheet. One of these is for an HPP. The other one belongs to a lowly C.E.

PHONE SHEET A:

NAME	PHONE	MESSAGE
Brian Grazer	310-555-9821	Pitching remake of *Grease* [Greasier]. Must buy.
CAA Partner	424-288-2000	Give Benicio his double-wide trailer already
Biz Manager	310-555-8879	How did you spend $20K at Kinara??
Brett Ratner	310-555-6666	Needs $5M more for budget or no movie
Sister	732-555-0911	Why aren't you calling Mom back?
French Consulate	011-33-777-77	Movie idea. Let's chat. Audrey T. likes.
Candy	818-555-0123	Great meeting you at Crazy Girls.
Travel Agent	310-555-7428	Vegas bachelor party will cost $70K/person.
Fiancé	310-555-9157	Some girl Candy called the house (third call)
Halle Berry	601-555-8366	"I have to play mountain woman in Nepal part."
Mom	732-555-9813	Why aren't you calling me back?
Chairman	x3800	Explain this $40M marketing budget memo
Melissa (ex)	323-555-8213	I think we should get back together.
Julia Roberts	310-555-2121	"I have to play mountain woman in Nepal part."
Steven Spielberg	818-555-9342	Passing on *Attila the Hun*
Sean Penn	310-555-0421	Invite w/Robin Wright to Fri dinner party
Dr. Mulligan	310-555-0911	Refill Paxil

In	L/W *	NTC **	Date	Time
●			Nov 11	2:22p
●			Nov 11	2:21p
●			Nov 11	2:21p
●			Nov 11	2:21p
●			Nov 11	2:20p
●			Nov 11	2:20p
●			Nov 11	2:19p
●			Nov 11	2:10p
●			Nov 11	2:07p
●			Nov 10	2:03p
●			Nov 3	10:00a
	●		Nov 11	2:23p
	●		Nov 11	11:30a
	●		Nov 11	9:03a
	●		Nov 7	9:00a
		●	Nov 11	11:30a
		●	Nov 11	12p

*L/W = Left Word; **NTC = Need To Call*

PHONE SHEET B:

NAME	PHONE	MESSAGE
Lou at CAA	424-288-2000	Client needs his check or his kids won't have Xmas.
Jane at HBO	323-555-8732	Great drinks. Want to join Girl's Bowling League?
Landlord	818-555-1578	Where's the rent check? Not afraid to evict.
Best Friend Julie	323-555-1432	Mani Pedis later? Don't tell Ross.
Gay Best Friend Ross	323-555-8111	Mani Pedis later? Don't tell Julie.
Sister	919-555-1211	FedEx your purple dress—need for wedding
Cousin Fred	646-555-8712	Stop flooding my inbox with cheesy forwards
Becca @ Barneys	310-555-8911	Spoke to manager and I can give sale price on shoes if you bring in receipt.
Larry	818-555-8103	Met you speed-dating. Dinner Sat?
Mom	919-555-0122	Buy Xmas ticket? Dad and I will pay for it. Please come.
President of Co.	x4011	Where are my notes on *Christmas with Papa*?
Agent at UTA	310-273-6700	Great spec—"Scarface meets Tootsie"
Dr. Bose	310-555-9900	Test results in. Must talk.
Ex Ian	917-555-7899	Stop calling and hanging up. Better yet, stop calling.

So, which phone sheet belongs to the HPP and which belongs to the C.E.?
Answer: We're not even going to dignify it with one.

In	L/W	NTC	Date	Time
●			Nov 11	12:01p
●			Nov 11	10:02a
●			Nov 11	9:45a
●			Nov 11	9:30a
●			Nov 11	9:28p
●			Nov 10	7:01p
●			Nov 9	12:22p
●			Nov 8	10:02a
●			Nov 7	3:30p
●			Nov 7	10:43a
	●		Nov 11	2:22p
	●		Nov 11	11:58a
	●		Nov 11	9:30a
	●		Nov 10	11:01p

Eavesdrop with Caution

"That bastard is the biggest a-hole producer I've ever dealt with. And I heard he slept with his second-cousin—Wait, are you sure the line is clear?"

AS A RULE, YOUR BOSS WILL NEED TO VENT to you. After all, the Biz can take a toll on an HPP if he's unable to release the stress and tension he accumulates during a typical day. That's where you come in.

So you know, your new job requires that you listen on every single one of your boss's calls. Eavesdropping is part of your new job (one you'll grow to love, BTW). Why does all of Hollywood do it? Because you have to be in your boss's loop in order to set meetings, prioritize tasks, and take notes on stealth conversations. (These come in handy when the boss gets subpoenaed for a crime he "didn't" commit. Google Anthony Pellicano for more on that.) More importantly, listening in allows you and your boss to bond.

You see, as the silent partner in this arrangement, your boss will often feel the need to follow up a particularly harrowing call by venting to you. She'll say things like, "I can't stand that jerk!" or "Can you believe anyone is that stupid?" or "I can't wait till she gets fired, should be any day now."

The boss knows she can speak so freely, however, because she assumes you have cleared the line. One of the worst possible mistakes you can make in your early days as an assistant is to *not* drop the third-party caller. Most phone systems have a "drop button," whereby you can disconnect the third person on the line but continue to stay on the line with your bossity boss. Use this. Or even better, hang up with your boss after every call, thus killing the old line, and call him right back so he can resume his tirade. Like abstinence, this is your only surefire way to guarantee safe venting. Which brings us to a fave funny story . . .

Hugo, whose boss was busy carving moguls in Telluride, took a call from a very high-powered agent and his Dumb Assistant. "Sorry, Janice is out of town on business," Hugo said. "I'll have her call back." At which point the call should have been over. Not so fast. Dumb Assistant, bless her soul, did not use the drop button. Hugo stayed on the line for the *next two hours* while Dumb Assistant and her boss rolled calls. Hugo got to learn about the director's deal they were making at Warners, the secret **spec** Keanu liked, and the agent's hefty divorce settlement (it seems said agent cheated on his wife with not only another woman but another man, both of whom happened to be his assistants). Needless to say, Hugo was thoroughly entertained and to this day he's waiting for the perfect opportunity to use this information to his advantage. When in Shadywood . . .

P.S. We almost forgot, another one of our all-time favorite amateur mistakes is forgetting to mute oneself. Please, when listening in on the call to the studio chief, make certain that no one can hear you tell the assistant next to you: "Ew! For the life of me I have no idea why they want to put Jude in that movie. Buncha dummies running this town . . ."

YOUR NEW BFF . . .

Is a little gadget called the **cordless headset.** Please, whatever you do, convince your company to invest. Because it's not only handsets that should be exiled from the face of the earth but also headsets with a cord. You do remember that scene where Nia Vardalos clotheslines herself in *My Big Fat Greek Wedding,* right? 'Cause we think they stole that idea from us.

Below find a picture of our chosen model: Plantronics CS70. We call him "Savior." You don't have to be stuck at your desk to answer the phone with this doohickey (although, since you've already put Rule 20 into action and made your cube a home, maybe you're happy to be stuck there).

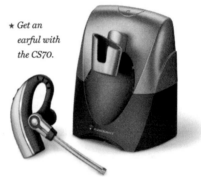

★ *Get an earful with the CS70.*

Okay, the truth is that this headset allows you to wander only a few yards away, but those few yards make a big difference when there's a full bladder involved. (Yes, 'tis true, we have answered the phone while in the loo.) Point is, get yourself a cordless so you can go on with your bad self and hit on Tammy 20 yards down the hall, *all while still manning the phones.*

P.S. Remember to take the headset off before you leave the office each night. Walking into your drinks at the Four Seasons with Savior on your ear is not a fashion statement you want to be making.

Less Is More

"I lost him in the canyon."

IF YOU'VE FOUND YOURSELF PUTTING AS MUCH thought into answering the phones as you do breathing, it means you're becoming the cream of the assistant crop. Nice work. As a result, a newfound confidence should now be starting to creep into the rest of your working life. But before we get too big for our britches, people, here's a little lesson on *how to dispense information over the phone*. The headline? Don't give people the kitchen sink. Look at the following scenario, for example:

Caller: Can I speak to fancy pants please? We have to get this deal done today.

You: I can't reach him today.

Caller: It's an emergency.

You: I'm sorry, he's completely out of contact.

Caller: I said emergency. Where is he?

You: On an island in the tropics with no cell service.

Caller: Listen you little . . . You tell me where he is or I'm going to hold you personally responsible for the 40 mill I'm going to lose unless you put him on the phone!

You: Okay, okay. He's staying at that hotel where Brad and Jen broke up. It's 32 miles due west of Turks and Caicos. He's in the King Coconut suite which, if you can believe, is more than my yearly salary. Why don't I just give you the direct dial . . .

There is only one thing that bothers us more than the assistant who gives away TMI over the phone though, and that is what we like to call the Canyon Lie. Pay attention.

Say you and your big-time boss are holding for a small-time producer when your boss, too bored to wait any longer, takes another call. Or jumps into an important meeting. Or just finds some better use of his time at that instant (to practice his golf swing, for example). Two seconds later the producer jumps on the phone and you are forced to make up some lame excuse for the shameless call dumping. L.A., with its sprawling highways and canyons, lends itself to the following:

"Shoot, you know what? He's in the car and I just lost him in the canyon. We'll get you right back."

Please, please don't say this. You see, the Canyon Lie is so overused and abused that, even if your boss's cell *does* cut out while driving through one, it's better to make up a new lie. Instead try: "His pregnant wife just called on the other line," or "She just stepped into her board meeting," or, best of all, the simple truth, "I don't have him. We'll try you back."

P.S. Along with the Canyon Lie, here are two others to avoid at all costs:

- "He's behind closed doors." This reeks of BS and lacks creativity. We know you can do better.

- "I'm sorry, but there has been a personal emergency." Really, invoking the "personal emergency" is about as bad as claiming your grandmother, happy and healthy down in Boca, died in order to get a few days off from work. You're just inviting bad karma into your life. And believe you me, you're gonna need good karma after working in this town for a few months.

Beware the Crazies

"310, 323, 212, and when feeling really generous, 818. Any other area code is not worth my time."

PEOPLE LOVE HOLLYWOOD. THEY REALLY DO. The glitz, the glamour, the knockdown drama between the paparazzi and the starlets they stalk.

That's why it's no surprise when you get one of *these* callers. The people whom we will refer to as crazies from here on out. You know them. They are the people who find your number in some Internet database and start calling. Daily. Some examples: the screenwriter in Anchorage who just sold her grandmother's final piece of bone china in order to support her "craft." The independent producer who claims James Cameron stole the idea for *Titanic* from him. And our favorite, the "old friend from grade school" who wants your boss to green-light his $200 million movie. In a perfect world, God would miraculously route all of these calls directly to voicemail. If you're so unlucky to have picked up, however, this is what you do:

First, keep it short. Remain professional, curt, and consistent. Never give the person on the other end the chance to pitch his screenplay. If you do, put the phone on hold and come back a few hours later. He might even be on act 2 by then.

Second, invoke the lawyers. "We can't take any unsolicited submissions. Any further inquiries will have to be directed to our legal department." Never mind that the legal department consists of your intern Zach, who dropped out of USC law school after two weeks.

Third, gather the troops. Every once in awhile you'll get lucky with these calls. "Hi. My name is Huey and I found your number online. I want to tell you about a project that will alter the universe and the way we as humans exist. It's called *Iraq: The Musical . . .*" This is when you resort to that wonderful invention called speakerphone. Every office needs an occasional, good laugh so why not invite all your coworkers to come join the fun? Who knows, maybe it will bring you and your fellow assistants that much closer. Until tomorrow, that is.

Last but not least, call security. Sometimes a crazy will be so nuts that he'll figure out a way to somehow sneak onto the lot and walk right into your office.

"Hi, I'm Stan Taylor, writer and director extraordinaire. I just drove two days straight to get here for my meeting with your boss. Is she ready for me?"

This actually happened to us, btw. What did we do? Locked ourself in the bathroom and called the police. Like we said, CRAZY.

MEMOIRS FROM THE MAILROOM:
THE LOONY LETTER

Many crazies take a different approach to breaking into Hollywood. Yes, we're talking about the **blind submission letter.** This is when a struggling screenwriter tries to pitch his brilliant movie idea in a letter. Assistants open dozens of these every day. You can see why we felt the need to share the sample below . . .

Dear Mr.(Name Spelled Wrong):

I read recently that your company produced that movie about the sinking blimp which, too bad for you, sank your studio. I mean, what were you thinking? $200 million and not one bona fide movie star? Anyway, my point is, I think you are missing out on what the American public really wants. What is that, you say?

My independently minded yet supremely commercial script is called COWGIRLS AND CYBORGS. C&C blends both the Western and Sci-Fi genres in a way that we've never seen before. Our heroine, Dusty Stargazer, is out galloping around the solar system on her cyborg horse (Clyde) when she comes across a conspiracy to end the human race as we know it. Lucky for the interplanetary United Nations and humans everywhere, Dusty has a few fighting tricks up her sleeve—and we're not just talking about that super duper laser shooter! What happens? You're on the edge of that seat thirsting for more? Well you'll just have to read the script, won't you?!

Oh, and I almost forgot, I got word yesterday that Jennifer Garner's people are interested in the Dusty role for her. (My rich cousin goes to the same manicurist in Park City where Jen goes when she's in town.)

Please check YES on the postcard I've included and I will send a copy of the script priority mail right away!

Sincerely,
Dick Dinkelheimer

Keep a Clean Calendar

"Let's see—how does 3:15 on April 11, 2087 sound?"

NEXT TO THE PHONES, THE SCHEDULE WILL BE your biggest responsibility in the office. You'll need to keep a precise calendar of all appointments in your boss's life, as well as the appointments for your boss's spouse, kids, ex-wives, and pet poodle Snookums. "Big whoop," you say. "In high school I managed the schedule for my parents' restaurant, which had 40 employees. I think I can handle one little executive . . ."

Oh no, you did not just say that. Really. You don't understand. Hollywood types are the most overbooked bunch of type-A's you're going to meet. A free ten minutes in the day means that, uh oh, business is lagging. "Aaron!! Why is there nothing scheduled before my lunch?" "Um, lunch starts in ten minutes." "And your point??"

You'll need to fit a 30-minute meeting into a 10-minute slot, squeeze a visit to little Kenny's soccer game between trips to Vancouver, and wrangle 25 people from all sides of town for an impromptu meeting that will start in, oh, look at that, 12 minutes ago.

What's even worse is that the schedule will be in constant flux. The schedule is never done for the day, even when the day is over. You'll have to cancel meetings five minutes before they start and somehow keep the writer who drove all the way from Orange County appeased when he hears about it. One of your favorite jokes will be, after having rescheduled a meeting with someone 14 times, scheduling a time for a reschedule. "Oh, and you'll lie. Especially when cancelling a meeting at the last minute. You'll use an excuse like "staff meetings with the partners" to cancel when, in reality, your boss just wants to take a nap. Another personal fave is, "Dear friend, things have gone terribly awry. I wish I could say more, but well . . . (insert huge long melodramatic sigh) . . . I can't." Create an air of mystery and the cancelee won't even fixate on the canceled meeting.

"What happens if my boss is the guy that keeps getting canceled on? How do I make this meeting finally happen??" Well, first off, *don't* be the assistant who calls nonstop to "like check in to, like, see if you, like, found a time for him to, like, stop by yet?" Send an e-mail instead. Chances are the other assistant is by virtue of having a busier boss, way busier than you. They still don't respond? Keep sending friendly reminders. Even better if you can make these reminders funny and self-deprecating. Be the assistant who "gets it"—that is, that knows their boss is a pariah that no one wants to meet with, *and* makes fun of it.

"HOW DO I STAY ON TOP OF THE SCHEDULE?"

■ **Live in the future.** This means, on Tuesday, think about next Tuesday. The one way to stay ahead of schedule, and keep people from hating your boss, is to prepare ahead.

■ **Maintain good records.** Chances are your calendar will be a million moving targets. The only way to keep track of them all is to note exactly how many times a meeting has been canceled and who has canceled on whom. That way when Boss Man asks, "How many times have we rescheduled Jesus?" you won't even have to think before you say, "Seven, and I have a feeling he might not appreciate eight."

■ **Forget about a personal life.** Let's face it, your own social calendar is going to suffer in this job, so stop pretending you have one and focus on your boss's instead.

■ **Keep a hard copy.** Sure, technology is great and all, but computers tend to break down just as your boss wants to go over the calendar. Print out the schedule at least once a day.

■ **The battle of the titans.** Every big meeting will involve at least three big egos. Coordinating their schedules is a nightmare. How to deal? Pack rations. You're gonna be scheduling this one for weeks.

A TYPICAL DAY IN HELL-AY:

No one understands just how busy a typical HPP is until they see their actual calendar. As such, we've included the below sample day in one such HPP's life. We're not kidding.

Tuesday, March 14

5:30 A.M.	Wake up to the koi fountain outside. Pretend to meditate. Down **Americano #1**.
5:40 A.M.	Pilates in the clubhouse with Ursula.
7:00 A.M.	Shower/Have assistant read Ridley script over speakerphone
7:15 A.M.	Jean-Michael does hair. **Americano #2**.
7:30 A.M.	Kiss the kiddies good-bye before Rubia takes them to school.
7:35 A.M.	Get in Mercedes. Don't forget spiritual healing CD for ride.
8:00 A.M.	Arrive at Peninsula for Oprah breakfast. **Americano #3**. (Reminder: Don't eat!)
9:30 A.M.	Roll calls on way to office/Pick up McMuffin at drive-thru.
10:00 A.M.	Script meeting with Ridley et al. **Americano #4**.
11:00 A.M.	Excuse self from Ridley meeting.
11:10 A.M.	Arrive late to budget meeting with the Germans. Seem flustered, then composed.
11:30 A.M.	Roll calls. **Americano #5**.
12:00 P.M.	General meeting with that slutty actress from MTV reality show.
12:15 P.M.	Get on phone for therapy conference call.
1:00 P.M.	Have phone "accidentally" cut out on therapist.
1:01 P.M.	Arrive virtually on time for lunch with L.A. *Times* journalist at The Grill. (Don't forget to nod to Sumner. NO carbs, only a bite of bibb lettuce.) **Americano #6**.
2:30 P.M.	Car, roll calls, stop at drive-thru for Big Mac.
3:00 P.M.	Marketing meeting. **Americano #7**. Try to stay awake.
4:00 P.M.	Staff meeting. Yell at them for lack of **tentpoles**.
4:45 P.M.	Call kiddies. Ask about Victoria's math test. Or was it French? **Americano #8**.
5:00 P.M.	Screen tests for that werewolf movie I don't know why we're making.

5:30 P.M.	Conference call with director of werewolf movie. **Americanos #9 and #10**.
6:15 P.M.	30-second shower/Maggie mists tan.
6:30 P.M.	Read speech for tonight's premiere for first time.
6:35 P.M.	Have breakdown about poorly written speech.
6:40 P.M.	Everyone to pump ego by commenting on how svelte I look in Armani suit.
6:45 P.M.	Get in car. **Americano #11**.
7:00 P.M.	Arrive at Chinese Theatre/Walk red carpet/Use potty.
7:30 P.M.	Screening starts. Only 30 mins late. Give speech.
7:40 P.M.	Sneak out of theatre. Stop at drive-thru for Big Mac #2.
8:10 P.M.	Get home in time to tuck kiddies into bed/Read story about absentee father.
8:30 P.M.	Massage with Hans/Don't wake wife.
9:00 P.M.	Back in limo.
9:30 P.M.	Arrive at Spago for premiere party. Whiskey sours #1 – 8.
10:00 P.M.	Sneak out Spago's back door.
10:30 P.M.	Read Oliver script/Late night run for Big Mac #3.
12:00 A.M.	Sleep/Respond to e-mails/Worry about lack of tentpoles/Ask God to make me not imbibe Americanos and/or frequent drive-thrus tomorrow.

Okay, maybe we're kidding . . . But only a little.

★ *HPPs have two essential food groups.*

Write Stuff Down

"Order Joan's for lunch, then call John at the gym, write a letter to Jim, I loved your movie, you crack me up, what about resurrecting the Ace Ventura franchise, et cetera, messenger it right over, and why isn't John already on the phone?"

AH, THE LAUNDRY LIST OF TO-DOS SHOUTED from your boss's mouth at the speed of a rapid-fire machine gun. In a sane world, you would always be able to ask your boss to repeat himself, just in case you didn't get it all down the first time. Unfortunately, this is Crazywood, which leads us to our next wise discovery: pen and paper.

No matter how fast technology advances, it will forever annoy us that they haven't figured out a way to improve our memory. Cutting back on the binge drinking would help there, but let's be real. Until scientists invent a chip for our brains we will continue to stand by the tried-and-true technique known as writing stuff down. This is one you learned in second grade, kiddos. Really, you should try it. You will forever have a task list to remind you of the things that you must do and a source of laughter for those things that you never intend on doing.

Believe us, being a successful assistant is in the details. Getting down Wolfgang Petersen's German mobile number before he cuts out is fine work. Scribbling a 1 instead of a 7 is not. Shipping that gift basket of the birthday bubbly to the A-list actress so it gets to Sydney on her birthday? You're brilliant! Yeah, not so much so when your boss reminds you she just joined AA. The notebook will help you prevent these fatal errors.

THE GUIDELINES OF NOTE TAKING:

- **Handcuff notebook to self.** Boss calls you into the office? Don't you dare walk in there without something to write on. After all, you're not 15—it's no longer okay to write on your hand.

- **No more scribbles.** When you've completed a task, rather than crossing it out with ink, simply go over it with your favorite color highlighter. Besides being easier on the eyes, this also allows you to go back and read over the phone number, dollar amount, or strange name (Boaty Boatwright? Yes, she is a real agent) that you wrote down a few days earlier.

- **Don't trash old notebooks.** You'll need to refer back to old notes. Your boss will be impressed when you can give her proof that you really did send Nicole Kidman's agent that female vampire script back in August of '06.

A HOLLYWOOD ARTIFACT

Our friend, assistant to a major HPP at one of the top-tier agencies, lent us this old page from her notebook.

- Send Wes Anderson script to Keanu.
- Flowers to Jennifer at 4 Seasons / KONA
☆ NOW! Set drinks w Harvey
- Book conference room for Mother Teresa biopic lunch
  Cate B. likes Chinese
  Order Mr. Chows
- Globetrotters project meeting invite: Harry, Bob, Lenny, Sue, Rachel, Kathy, and the guy who directed Hoosiers
☆ Get Scarlett J. her check!

Bite Your Tongue

"I hate you."

AT THIS POINT YOUR BOSS HAS SCREAMED AT you, thrown staplers, blamed you for things out of your control, and made you clean up Lulu the chihuahua's "accident." And this is one of your better days. But you're close to cracking now.

"Just this once, I beg of you. Tell me it's okay to tell this mofo exactly what I think."

Sorry, child, we hate to censure you, but it's never okay to talk back to the boss.

Trust us, we've known those who've let loose with their tongue and let's just say that they still haven't recovered from the subsequent trauma. (Think upended Eames chair, them still in it.)

"But," you whine, "what happens if they are really out of line?"

Very funny. Like your boss is ever out of line.

Here's the deal. Sometimes, maybe even more than sometimes, you will be ethically, emotionally, and physically justified in talking back to your boss. However, doing so will rarely get you what you want. Rather it's better to display a calm mind and even-keeled temper. It is precisely in these moments that your boss will be impressed with your ability to handle his craziness (yes, he does know he's crazy), and all of your coworkers will marvel at your people skills. Before long, people across town will be talking about you as the martyr that you have legitimately become. Directors will want you on their sets. Other agents—partners even—will poach you. Hell, Queen Elizabeth might even knight you.

"But what do I do with all my pent up resentment?" Go ballistic on your keyboard. That's right, purge your anger with friends via instant message. You'll be surprised how much better you'll feel once you've gotten that out of your system.

If that doesn't work, take it out on your roommates, or, even better, your mother. Okay, never on Mom. Try competitive sports instead. Hockey, boxing, roller derby—these will help release your frustrations. Oh, and sex might help too.

Our final word of advice: If it gets really bad—and we're talking blood spilled, psychotic thoughts, or even just one too many crying sessions—you can always sue. Sure, you'll never work in this town again, but it won't matter when you're sipping caipirinhas on the beach in Ipanema.

THE NEW WATERCOOLER

Thank god for technology. Before such things as instant messaging and anonymous blogging, assistants had to keep their evil thoughts to themselves. Things have changed though, and in any given day in Hollywood entire encyclopedias are being written about bad bosses. And we truly feel that this new way to complain has led to an overall healthier Assistant State of Mind. Because instead of having to keep our evil thoughts bottled up until our nightly bitchfest session at St. Nicks,* assistants can now purge their venom the very second it happens. What can we say? Venting makes us feel better, which makes us work better.

For example, little does the Bad Boss at CAA know that, as he screams obscenities, you are busy transcribing the entire tirade word for word to your friend who works as a math teacher up in Seattle. What about venting to your industry friends? Not smart. Even though it's okay for you to commiserate with your friend at Universal, you don't want to do this *in writing*. Otherwise, risk having your little tirade finding its way to Defamer.

ANOTHER WARNING! Although unlikely, there is the possibility of a suspicious boss having the tech guy dig up old instant message files on your computer. So, yes, bitch at your own risk. But if you've learned your rules, why would he suspect you?

St. Nicks is a dive bar that will remind you of home. Come here for greasy fries and easy conversation (8450 W. Third St. at La Cienega; 323-655-6917).

Expense Honestly

"Don't forget to expense that pack of gum I bought from CVS today."

THERE'S A DIRTY LITTLE SECRET IN HOLLYWOOD that no one wants you to know. Many of the mega wealthy in this business are also mega cheap.

You know all those stories you hear about celebrities shopping at their favorite stores for free? And the gynormous gift baskets they give away at the Oscars, containing plane tickets to the Maldives that will sit unused for all eternity? Well, they're all true. The rich get richer, and we're not talking spiritually. One reason for this is a marvelous little invention called the **expense account.** As an assistant, you will be required to keep tabs on all of your boss's receipts. That means you'll have to distinguish between the personal and the business ones. Take it from us, this is a very murky line.

For example, consider the Mastro's* dinner with the studio chief who is also your boss's best friend. Chances are they will spend most of the dinner gossiping about the actors they'd like to hook up with or the business associates they'd like to see fall flat on their faces. Doesn't sound like business, right? Wrong. The ingenious thing about working in entertainment is that everything entertaining can be expensed. The movie ticket from last weekend? Check. The iPod necessary for listening to books on tape during that flight to Park City? Check. The three-week stay in Maui where your boss, ahem, "held writer meetings?" Well, um, you probably shouldn't expense *all* of that one. At least not the Lomi Lomi Massage with Margarita from Spa Services. "But she pitched me her female superhero idea throughout the whole thing!" your boss might argue. Sure, try and explain that one to the shareholders.

The worst part about having to keep track of every meal, gadget, and facial that your insatiable boss will purchase is that you rarely get any of the freebies. Believe us, you tend to get a tad bit resentful expensing $1,000 lunches when the last free meal you got was the one your roommate's mom bought you at IHOP. Don't fret. Someday you too will have an expense account. Just promise us you'll show some self-control and refrain from having corporate pay for your personal trainer, to whom you "gave acting advice" while pressing ten-pound dumbbells.

Mastro's Steakhouse (246 N. Canon Drive; 310-888-8782) is a staple of the power set. Book a table here for your promotion celebration, or catch a happy hour drink upstairs by the piano bar. Beware though, money is no object for most of the regulars here. Save splurging on the live Maine lobster for the really special occasions.

Risa's FIRST WIVES CLUB 2 set visit

RECEIVED OF PETTY CASH
No. _____ DATE 1/18 Risa
DESCRIPTION OF ITEM / SERVICE PURCHASED | AMOUNT
AVJET | $65,000.—
Flight to New York
CHARGE TO ACCOUNT

RECEIVED OF PETTY CASH
DATE 1/18
DESCRIPTION OF ITEM / SERVICE PURCHASED | AMOUNT
Mercer Hotel/Diane Keaton | $88 65
purpose:
to convince to stay in
movie—
INTENT | TOTAL 88 65

RECEIVED OF PETTY CASH
No. _____ DATE 1/18
DESCRIPTION OF ITEM / SERVICE PURCHASED | AMO
Four Seasons
Bette Midler
PURPOSE: to FIRE
FROM MOVIE—

RECEIVED OF PETTY CASH
No. _____ DATE 1/8
DESCRIPTION OF ITEM / SERVICE PURCHASED | AMOUNT
Elaines/ Uma Thurman | $689 31
PURPOSE:
To Pitch Grocery Checker
Project
Risa | TOTAL 689 31

RECEIVED OF PETTY CASH
No. _____ DATE 1/8
DESCRIPTION OF ITEM / SERVICE PURCHASED | AMOUNT
Yellow CAB | $176 54
Steven Spielberg
JURASSIC PARK 8 meeting
in Hamptons | TOTAL 176
CHARGE TO ACCOUNT
Risa
RECEIVED BY | APPROVED BY
FORM 3008 | MADE IN U.S.

DUANE READE
Altoids in prep for
meeting with
Steven | $1
CHARGE TO ACCOUNT | TOTAL $1 95
Risa
RECEIVED BY | APPROVED BY
TOPS FORM 3008 | MADE IN U.S.A.

RECEIVED OF PETTY CASH
No. _____ DATE 1/19
DESCRIPTION OF ITEM / SERVICE PURCHASED | AMOUNT
Hot Dog Vendor | $1 00
* Lunch on set
Risa
ACCOUNT
RECEIVED BY

RECEIVED OF PETTY CASH
DATE 1/19
DESCRIPTION OF ITEM / SERVICE PURCHASED | AMOUNT
PURPOSE: MUSIC EXPRESS
AIRPORT | $390 90
CARS
Risa | TOTAL $390 90
ACCOUNT
RECEIVED BY | APPROVED BY
3008

RECEIVED OF PETTY CASH
No. _____ DATE 1/19
DESCRIPTION OF ITEM / SERVICE PURCHASED | AMOUNT
American Air | $8871 32
Flight Home
Risa | TOTAL 8871 32
CHARGE TO ACCOUNT
RECEIVED BY | APPROVED BY
TOPS FORM 3008 | MADE IN U.S.A.

RECEIVED OF PETTY CASH
DATE 1/19
DESCRIPTION OF ITEM / SERVICE PURCHASED | AMOUNT
Candy B/W
Hot Tamales
for flight | .75
Risa | TOTAL .75
CHARGE TO ACCOUNT
RECEIVED BY | APPROVED BY
TOPS FORM 3008 | MADE IN U.S.A.

GPS Now Stands for Great Production Secretary

IT'S 1:11 P.M. YOUR BOSS IS OFF TO LUNCH AND YOU HAVE SOME breathing room. Aah, you think, finally a bit of peace and quiet. Forty-nine blissful minutes to sip a Cup-a-Soup and glance at today's trades. Maybe you'll even e-mail that girl you met Friday night who works at Endeavor. And then that phone starts ringing. Crap.

Bosses in L.A. are notorious for getting lost. And really, it's not their fault. Some genius engineer decided not to design our city on a grid. Try using a map to find your way through the winding streets of the Hollywood Hills or the chaos that is Bel-Air and you'll see what we mean. And please, don't get us started on the Bermuda Triangle (aka the Valley). But that's bygones. All it means is that, even though you've resided here for only three months and know nothing but the 12-block radius around your crappy apartment, your boss is still going to expect you to function as a human MapQuest. Do you know every possible right and wrong turn between your office and that new restaurant three blocks north of Barneys? No?

Well, neither do we. What we do know is how to be resourceful. Here are a few time-tested techniques for solving the pervasive lost-in-L.A. problem.

■ **The Bible:** Buy a *Thomas Guide* and use it (www.thomas.com). Although overwhelming at first, this book will act as your guide in times of crisis. Especially when the Internet is down and MapQuest has abandoned you.

■ **The Native:** Seek out the assistant who has lived in L.A. his or her entire life. Make sure you have their IM, cell phone, and office numbers on speed dial for when you need coordinates for that new dinner hot spot in some random canyon.

■ **The Cheat:** Who else is going wherever your boss is headed? Call that person's assistant, make friends, and get a copy of their directions (networking and getting directions, two points for you!).

■ **The Explorer:** Check out different brunch places on the weekend, visit those cousins in Los Feliz, and shop for furniture in Venice. Only by exploring will you figure out what is west of Bundy, north of Sunset, and south of the 110. *Then* comes Pasadena.

"Part of working in the mailroom at this agency was delivering scripts to the clients at night. Why waste money on messenger fees when you've got a bunch of employees with their own cars willing to drive around the city for minimum wage? Yeah, it sucked, especially since it was raining on that particular night. (Yes, it rains in L.A. Don't believe the whole 'sunny, 80-degree weather all the time' thing.) The actress who needed the script lived in the Silver Lake Hills which, from experience, is a road rage incident waiting to happen. My used '92 Nissan practically dropped its engine trying to get up those rain-slicked hills. Finally I found the house. I left my car running, got out, and chucked the package at the front door. It wasn't until I went to get back in the car that I realized I locked myself out. With the engine still running

TRUE CONFESSIONS

and cell phone sitting on the passenger seat. The only option was to knock on the actress's door, use her phone, and wait in the rain for AAA. Which I tried to do. She wouldn't let me wait outside, you see. I tried to refuse, not because I'm polite but because I thought her agent would find out what an idiot I was and fire me the next day. She wouldn't hear it though. So for the next hour I sat on the sofa with the actress and her brother watching *Dawson's Creek*. The fact that a few years later she'd star in a movie with Dawson himself still makes me laugh. Oh, and she even made me hot chocolate. The best part? The next day she told her agent that he should promote me. Two days later I was an assistant in the Lit department. I haven't messengered a script since."　　　　**—B.V.**

Book Travel with Care

"My friend and I are going fly-fishing at this river in Montana for a few days . . ."

YOUR BOSS IS GOING ON HIS TRI-ANNUAL vackay with his "college buddy," and you get to plan the big bad—but also very discreet—getaway. Time to brush up on your Internet searching abilities for five-star remote cabins in the wilderness, along with arranging all car pickups, flights, and hotels. Yes, it's not in the job description. Yes, it's ludicrous that you have to do it. But you best suck it up and make sure the boss gets his corner suite with the unlimited minibar access because no matter where you're working as an assistant, "travel agent" is now part of your job description.

Don't fret. Console yourself with the thought that somewhere in the depths of your being you have vowed never to treat any assistant the way you're being treated right now. (Even though you know at a still deeper level that you plan on having five assistants, one of whom will be completely devoted to personal travel.)

A FEW TRAVEL TIPS:

- **Make a travel agent your friend today.** You'd be surprised what rabbits they can pull out of their hat in times of crisis (e.g., that yellow Hummer our boss decided he had to have three hours before his excursion through the Amazon).

- **Foster your connections.** Send the girl at the Ojai Valley Inn a few DVDs. Invite the concierge at the Four Seasons to your studio's next New York premiere. Throw these people a Hollywood bone now and then and they'll be panting to help you out the next time.

- **Go the extra mile.** Did you offer to FedEx the boss's luggage so he wouldn't have to schlep it on that god-awful commercial flight? Have his weekend scripts reduced to four-by-six inches for a more compact carry-on size? Sanitizing Handi-Wipes placed in his satchel to combat those germs in the Town Car? Pack his favorite protein bars for the layover flight? Did you? Did you? Well, you should have.

- **Channel their stomach.** Boss getting in late from a cross-continental flight? Call room service and have that Chinese chicken salad (hold the carb-heavy wontons) waiting for her when she gets into the room. As a fun little bonus, this works well in your personal life too.

Think how your fiancée, traveling to Las Vegas for her third trade show of the month, will feel when she finds you've left her a welcome gift at her hotel. You just might get lucky.

ON LOCATION:

The Movie Business, like many industries learning to prosper in this global economy we've got going here, does business in cities around the world. Therefore, you will now be booking nonstop set visits for your globetrotter boss. To quote Julie Andrews, these are a few of our favorite things:

- **HOTEL:** Four Seasons. In every glam locale, and their high-class service is what your high-class boss will demand. (www.fourseasons.com)

- **CAR:** Music Express can book a sedan in any city at anytime. (800-255-4444; www.musiclimo.com)

- **JET:** Boss too VIP to fly commercial? Book a private jet at www.bluestarjets.com. After one too many trips back and forth from Australia with the two screaming babies in first class, you should maybe convince the boss to get a jet share at www.netjets.com. Or

---

TRUE CONFESSIONS

"At that point I'd worked in the movie business for like five years and had never set foot on a set. My boss was a pretty prolific producer but that didn't mean he let me leave my desk. So he's down in Australia doing this dumb action film and I was like, screw it, I'm going to ask if I can go visit. And he said yes. I know, I was just as shocked. So I flew down there on his miles (economy) and by the time we land I've got like 20 voicemails from him. Which was normal. What wasn't was that they were all about the same thing. He wanted me to plan this romantic dinner in his suite. No, not for me. For his new chica who, of course, was starring in the film. So I plan the dinner in his suite—three courses, some candles, lots of alcohol, whatever. By the time I finish, the movie's done shooting for the day. So I don't go to the set, realize I'm jet-lagged, and fall asleep. Next thing I know it's morning and my phone's ringing. My boss 'Thank you. You did an excellent job.' I couldn't speak. He'd never said that before so I knew he must have gotten laid and that was not something I wanted to be thinking about. So then I ask him if I can drive to the set with him later and he says, 'Actually, about that, do you mind catching the next flight back to L.A.? It kind of freaks me out not having you in the office.' I literally was on the next plane home." —**L.S.**

---

have him grab his own "private piece of the sky" as a Christmas gift for the mistress at www.skyjet.com. The spouse will never even know about that weekend jaunt to Paris for pains au chocolat and other sordid delights.

 CELL: Do yourself a favor. Make sure your boss's mobile will work across the globe. Renting international cells is very 1999. Besides, teaching your boss how to use a new phone when she can't even master the one she's had for the past year is not a good use of time.

CONCIERGE: Do you know who is in charge at every major hotel? God, we hope not. Better to convince your boss to sign up for an international VIP concierge service such as the one at www.quintessentially.com. Who else is going to drive two hours out of London to pick up that special macrobiotic broccoli at 11 P.M. on a Tuesday? You won't believe what you will need to get these people to do for you.

The Road to Success Is a Paper Trail

"Did you get a follow-up fax to the e-mail confirmation regarding that phone call double-checking the meeting location?"

SO YOU'VE ORDERED A MESSENGER TO TAKE the boss's superconfidential script to the superstar's house on Mulholland with the electrical fence, motion detectors, and two Doberman attack dogs. The package cannot be left, for fear that Colombian drug lords will come out of the bushes, steal the envelope, and distribute it in places as far as Bogotá because, according to your boss, the script is just that good. (We know, you read it and thought it was the biggest piece of crap since *Ishtar*. Not the point.)

You ask the messenger service for the name of the driver (José), with whom you speak directly. You demand a phone call once the script has been hand delivered to the assistant (Crystal), who will be waiting at the gate between 10:05 and 10:15. Crystal will call you verifying that the script has arrived. Phew. You are free to spend the rest of the afternoon scouring the Internet for pics of Heidi Klum. But then it happens. A sound so bloodcurdling they should record it for horror films.

"Roooooooooooooooobbbbbbieeeeeeeeeeeeeeeeee!!!!!!"

You scurry into Boss's office, whereupon he tells you that the superstar never got the script. "But I talked to his assistant and the messenger and they told me he did," you retort. Sucks for you that Crystal is unreachable and the messenger service fired José for illicit activities in the back of the van. You, my friend, are screwed. You didn't get written proof. Only an actual piece of paper can bail you out of a bad situation. Otherwise it's your word against the other guy's, and chances are your boss will automatically side with the latter.

Here are simple ways to verify your side of things:

■ **Use e-mail whenever possible.** As long as you don't delete e-mails, you'll have a system of authentication that can go years back.

■ **Ask for follow-up receipts.** When ordering gifts or supplies, make the vendor fax you the receipt. Until that piece of paper is in your hands, assume the job is not done. Keep calling until you get it.

■ **Print everything.** Even if it's an instant message, the written word trumps the spoken. Get proof on paper.

Everything else is just hearsay. And hearsay doesn't fly in the Hollywood court of law.

Cater Out

"Darling, honey, whatever your name is, could we get some crudités in this meeting? Or maybe some Japanese kumquats? Benicio is peckish."

FROM THIS POINT ON, YOU ARE RUNNING a five-star joint out of the corner of your desk that also doubles as the company kitchen. Espresso machine? Check. Hot plate? Check. A seasonal selection of organic teas? "Oh shoot, Miss Paltrow. I think I ran out of the Rooibos African Leaf. I knew I should have ordered a double shipment from my Senegali supplier."

Yep, you might as well have graduated from the Culinary Institute of America because chef is also part of your job description. Throw out the Ho-Hos, Hostess Snowballs, and Ding Dongs, as you have now entered the world of clean eating. Worse, you're now catering to some of the pickiest, highest-maintenance eaters this side of the vegan aisle at Whole Foods. How to minimize your stress? Here are some basics:

■ **Upsell the water.** Why? Because it's easy. It comes in a plastic container that requires absolutely no cleanup. Please see below scenarios for suggestions on how to—and how to *not*—receive your guests.

You: "Can I offer you a drink, Ms. Barrymore?"

Them: "Lemme see, what do you have back there? Wow, a Nespresso machine! Great then, I'll have a double no-caf latte, light on the foam, throw some hazelnut in it, and Carol here would love a . . ."

vs. . . .

You: "Can I get you some cool, crisp, refreshing, soul-purifying water imported from Fiji while you wait?"

Them: "Thanks!"

■ **Play supermarket sweep.** Is your eager-beaver intern annoying you? Have him take the corporate card and go shopping for some healthy fare at the local Trader Joe's. (Candy, after all, is for the weak of heart.) He can load up on all the snacks your boss—and you, porky—could ever want. And when someone asks, "Do you have any dried fruit?" you'll say "Raisins, apricots, peaches, mango, ginger, or a variety pack?"

- **Turn tea time into free time**. If you know there's a big meeting on the books in those daunting afternoon hours, for godsakes, be prepared. That means ordering that take-out meal from The Grill* way ahead of time. You don't want to be sweating bullets trying to find last-minute treats that will appease the cranky people who keep wandering out of your boss's 4 P.M. board meeting.

- **Eat up.** Try to eat at least two meals a day on the company dime. You get paid too little after all. So fill up on the freebies in your office's kitchen. Just avoid the trans fat.

TRUE CONFESSIONS

"Out of all the skills I thought I'd acquire during my time in Hollywood, I never expected 'salad-tossing' to be one of them. My first boss taught me well, though. He is part of that particular breed of Hollywood Power Player known as a manorexic. Every day, for the entire two years I worked for him, I made him a lunch consisting of forty spinach leaves, three ounces of tofu, five almonds, and a teaspoon of low-fat Hidden Valley Ranch, with half a Hershey's Kiss for dessert. When he had lunch out of the office, he'd eat the salad beforehand and then spend the whole meal at The Grill making jokes so that no one would notice that his prime rib sat untouched. A few weeks into the job I had the salad down to a science. I even started eating it myself and quickly lost twenty pounds. Too bad that starvation's not so good for your mental acuity. This one day, in what can only be described as a malnutrition-induced stupor, I dressed his salad with some full-fat bleu cheese my intern bought by accident. I apologized profusely, fired the intern, and even agreed to work weekends for the next year to make up for the mistake. Luckily the boss man didn't fire me—'But only because standing next to you makes me look thinner,' he said. That night I went straight to In 'N Out after work. Four cheeseburgers later (animal style) I was on my way back to my old fat self— just like the boss wanted me to be." **—H.R.**

What's The Grill? Only one of Beverly Hills' most famous power lunch spots. Corner booths are prime real estate, filled with the Clint Eastwoods and Rupert Murdocks of the world. Befriend the maître d', or end up on the chopping block . . . right near to your boss's medium-rare filet (9560 Dayton Way, Beverly Hills; 310-276-0615, www.thegrill.com).

Always Be in Touch

"in screenin . . . movie a snore. can u deliver pizza? Extra crisssppy crust. theater 4. me in back."

YOUR BOSS PROBABLY HAS A CRACKBERRY (ALSO known as the BlackBerry). If you're working for someone super-crazy and controlling, chances are *you* have a BlackBerry too. Now we've heard of those time-management courses that instruct people to check e-mail only once a day so as to remain productive and stress free. Guess what? These are people who don't work in Hollywood. Maybe at the library or perhaps the paint drying factory, but definitely not Hollywood.

Let's be clear: E-mail is no longer an aspect of life that you can review and respond to at your leisure. From now on, it is life. Love it or hate it, the BlackBerry is an in-your-face, screaming-bloody-murder, instant-information messenger that has now replaced the phone call. For instance a "pls grab me a Pellegrino, and Barb wants a cap" from your boss (who incidentally is sitting ten feet away from you) is meant to be read immediately. The "pushmy4pmto430" that gets sent at 3:47? What are you waiting for? Get on it!

Then there are those few paltry hours each day when you're not in the office and can give your BlackBerry a rest. NOT! Yup, what once first seemed like a cool thing to show off to your friends is now the ultimate life-suck. Your boss will be in touch with you 24/7. Believe us, there's nothing like waking up from a work nightmare at 5 A.M. only to see that damn thing flashing with 14 e-mails your boss sent at 3:23 A.M. (We know those who set the BlackBerry on the vibrate feature, sleeping with it on their chest, lest they miss an important middle-of-the-night message. This is where we draw the line.)

That said, if you have a boss who insists on being able to interrupt every waking moment of your life, may we point out that the BlackBerry is far superior to the dreaded cell phone option. We now direct your attention to two scenarios.

CELL PHONE VERSION:

Boss: "Jess? Sorry, I can't hear you too well. Are you still there? Good. Listen, what was the name of the kid whose brother went to film school, is my mom's family friend, and I watched his short and said I would read his script? What was his script called?"

VS. . . . .

BLACKBERRY VERSION:

"Kid. Came in, family friend of mom, we watched short, read script. What were the names of all those things?"

You get our drift. The BB gives you time to pause, think, and figure out how to solve your boss's dilemma. So, when forced to choose between these two evils, go with the BB and cherish your once-a-year BlackBerry-free vacation at a remote locale.* Please see the map for suggestions.

**SUITABLE LOCATIONS FOR
BLACKBERRY–FREE VACATIONS**

Serbia, Baghdad, The Congo, or try renting a cabin in the highest parts of ski resorts. We've also had luck in the middle of Lake Tahoe, parts of Nova Scotia, and five remote villages outside of Changsha, China.

"It's not like I was stupid or anything. It's just, well whatever, maybe I was a little stupid. It was my first job. I thought everyone slept with their boss. It was Hollywood after all. Which wouldn't have been that bad, but then I made the really, really stupid mistake of BlackBerrying this girl Rachel who I work with—all while my boss is sleeping right next to me. 'You'll never guess where I am right now,' that sort of thing. She responds, 'Where?' I respond back, giving her hints '. . . Underneath Frette sheets,' 'There's a photo of him and Spike Lee on the wall,' those types of things, until we've got like this 20 e-mail long chain going. As soon as she guesses who it is, I of course start panicking, begging her over e-mail not to say anything. Too late. Bitch had already forwarded the emails to this other coworker, who forwarded them to someone else and so on and so on. They couldn't fire me, but they did move me to a different office. Working for this creep in legal. Anyway, I quit a few weeks later. Working there was too weird and, well, I guess I just felt like an idiot. It's all good now though. I took this job in publicity and everyone here's got some similar horror story. I feel like a nun compared to these people." **—J.K.**

TRUE CONFESSIONS

Add "Chore Whore" to the Resume

"Girl! Oh giiiiirl! Yes, you, the chubby one. Can you come over here and hem this skirt?"

AS WE ONCE READ ON THE BACK OF A Starbucks cup, Gandhi said, "Be the change you want to see in the world." And we believe that sort of. However, there are some times when you're going to have to suck it up and *not* be the change. This means playing maid. In other words, we regret to inform you that the next time the boss says, "Quick, clean up my kid's vomit before it soaks into the afghan rug Stephen gave me for Christmas," you better have the paper towels ready.

Sorry kids, but being a maid is a standard part of being an assistant. Some of our friends have even been known to dust, wash windows, and fluff pillows while on the job.

"What about plunging a clogged toilet? Certainly you're not saying that's part of my job description."

Actually, we are, sorry. In fact, we've got quite a few pointers on how to give the toilet a good plunge. Take us out for a few drinks, and we might even share them with you.

That said, there are some duties that *only* a maid should perform. Here are some instances when things have gone too far:

A. "Where is the Façonnable baby blue shirt? Is it at the dry cleaners?"
"In your closet, right-hand side," you answer, because of course you know the whereabouts of the contents of your boss's closet. This is *not* okay in our book. Also out of bounds: washing, drying, and ironing in the office. That means no Spray 'n Starch in your desk drawer. You're not a laundromat.

B. "Did you forget to pick up my birth control pills?"
Never should you have any involvement whatsoever in your superior's reproductive life. "But what about shipping frozen breast milk in a sealed frozen container complete with dry ice?" Not okay. Neither is handling sperm donations or in vitro fertilization.

C. "Can you do me a favor and try on those low-rise panties for my wife? I'm not sure, but she's about the same size as you . . ."

It's time to consider the following response: "I'd like to help you, but do you think you could possibly check her drawer to see her size yourself? Besides, do you really want me knowing what her underwear looks like?" The point? You must draw the line between being the *office* domestic and the *house* domestic.

Other than these cases, you're going to need to endure a bit of servitude. But only because there's an opening at that hot production company and you're going to get the big-time recommendation from the boss since you just filled in for Consuela-the-lactating-nanny at last week's Mommy and Me. And when you're Boss? You *promise* to always BYOBM (Bring Your Own Breast Milk).

"When I started working for this actress, I knew I'd have to do some work on weekends. Personal assistants to celebs always had to. I was fine with it as long as I got overtime. That was before I found out that overtime meant spending every waking second of my life shopping for shoes. Sounds like fun, right? Not when your boss has freakishly enormous feet. For an entire year I dedicated my Saturdays to searching for size 10½ Jimmy Choos. And let me tell you something: Unless you're Sarah Jessica Parker, Jimmy doesn't make size 10½. My boss didn't care. I just needed to 'procure the shoes,' even if that meant stealing them from some old lady on the street. Well, I tried and tried, but never found them. I relayed the bad news to my boss, who insisted on following me to my next visit to Barneys. She went off on me in the middle of the store. 'Are you insinuating that I have big feet?' she screamed. 'Please don't tell me you were attempting to insult me, especially since you have the worst skin this side of the pizza parlor. . . .' The humiliation didn't end there. She proceeded to hurl every couture pump she could find down the Barneys stairwell. Let's just say our relationship ended there. By the way, my complexion has completely cleared up since I quit. Her feet? Still man-sized, I'm sure." **—D.M.**

TRUE CONFESSIONS

Zip It

"Of course my assistant is not on the phone."

AT THE BEGINNING OF YOUR TENURE AS A Professional Schlepper you will probably think it a tad ridiculous how important, time sensitive, and secretive everything in Hollywood seems to be. After all, you may think, "It's just a stupid spec script that no one's going to buy. What's the big deal if my room-mate knows how much our company bid?" Or, "Does anyone really care if Charlize demands an extra plane ticket for her mom in all of her contracts? That's a fun little frothy fact I'd really like to share with my own mom."

Yes, big mouth, people do care! And they'll stab you in the back to get this information. Especially since everyone knows, as we stated earlier, that assistants listen in on all calls. The point? If not careful, you could really screw over your boss and, inevitably, yourself.

Regardless of where you work, big or small, you are part of a team, and you need to be a team player if you want to get anywhere. If friends from other places needle you for information, always play dumb. "But didn't you guys get an offer for Clive Owen in that movie?" asks your new annoying acquaintance at Imagine. "Shoot, I don't know. I was stuck making a mochaccino for my boss so I didn't hear that call."

The point is, if you know sensitive information, and then go blabber it to your new best friend over brunch at Toast and she tells her big-time partner boss at 3 Arts, then *you* are toast. Just never give away the company secrets. At times your job may seem small and unimportant, but the information to which you are now privy is not. It's the stuff that makes Hollywood go around!

So, order your scooped-out bagel with lox and chat about Natalie Portman's latest movie, but do not mention how you are paying Mr.

Action Star double his last salary in that sequel that you happen to know is already $40 million over budget.

Do that and you're better suited for a job as Perez Hilton's assistant not the studio chief's.

EXCEPTIONS TO THE RULE:

Here are some secrets that you SHOULD divulge . . .

Hot spot restaurants: Big-time boss just told you that dinner at the remodeled Sofitel hotel Simon was, and we quote, "A salivatory orgasm." Tell all the friends to meet there for a great night on the town. May we suggest the junk food platter for dessert? It comes with cotton candy, a milkshake, and caramel corn. (8555 Beverly Blvd.; 877-240-3570)

Up and coming talent: Only after your boss has officially closed the deal with the brilliant new director who got Diane Lane to commit to his next flick is it okay to let the cat out of the bag and tell the friends to watch his tear-jerking documentary about the children of Rwanda.

Celebrity divorces: Are you the first to find out that America's It Couple is headed for Splitsville? Definitely tell everyone and their mother that you heard it first. I mean, you might as well just sell the story to *Access Hollywood.* Maybe they'll want you for an exclusive! No one will ever . . . *Just kidding.* This, naïve ones, is a definite "lips sealed for all eternity . . . or at least till it's on TMZ" secret.

DON'T STOP, IT GETS JUICIER!
BONUS ROUND AHEAD!

We are at the end of Assistant Boot Camp, folks. We know, you're feeling like this business is packed full of roadblocks. Please don't be discouraged; it's not how we want you to feel. After all, there is a great deal of fun to be had and, as far as perks go, Hollywood assistants have way more than any of those junior I-bankers on Wall Street, pages on Capitol Hill, and tech nerds in Silicon Valley. Here are just a few of the cherries to be plucked off the top of the delicious layer cake that is Perkwood:

! SWAG. As a rule, the haves in Hollywood will continue to have more than the have-nots. **Swag** (technical definition: "free crap!") can include everything from trademarked hats, visors, shirts, children's shoes with Disney characters on them, Cheerios boxes with cartoon tunas, a remote control car to promote your new flying car movie . . . you get the drift. P.S. Don't be the guy who thinks it's acceptable to wear an entire outfit made out of swag. We're talking, a *Spider-Man* T-shirt, *Harry Potter* sweatpants, and a *Pirates of the Caribbean* keychain, topped off with a *Deuce Bigalow* beanie. This isn't a college football game after all—there is such a thing as *too* much team spirit.

! GIFT BAGS. You've heard all about them I'm sure. Doled out at premieres and other VIP events, goodie bags can be filled with books, gadgets, or makeup from Sephora. We even scored a shuffle and gift card to iTunes one time. Yes, we were feeling very special.

! DVDs. From time to time, you'll be given DVDs, some of which will be unwatchable crap you yourself worked on. But at least you can regift them to distant cousins.

! BOOKS. If you work for an agent, you will probably get tons of books, and if you work for a producer you will probably be submitted tons of books. So read up and enrich your mind, perkhead.

! MOVIE PREMIERES. Depending on whom you work for (more powerful = more tix) you will get leftover movie premiere tickets. Chances are you won't be able to make the actual screening part (who gets out of work before 7:30, after all) but that doesn't matter because there's always time for the party. That means free booze, festive hors d'oeuvres, and a gift bag. You'll go to bed drunk, stuffed, and the owner of more junk than you had the night before.

! LEFTOVERS. Food is bountiful in Hollywood, mostly because all the world's top chefs flock to L.A., cooking up concoctions to make your gastrointestinal system go bust, but also because no one here truly eats. Point is, there will always be some restaurant gift certificate that you find in the bottom of your boss's desk drawer (ask before taking, of course) and even more leftover food from today's staff lunch. So even if you're not hungry, imagine the warm-and-fuzzies you'll get after donating those doggie bags to the downtown homeless shelter.

! WATER. You think we're kidding, but we're not. If all else fails, learn to appreciate the unlimited supply of bottled H_2O at your disposal. Most of the population on the globe drinks out of a creek and here you are with quarts and quarts of water imported from springs in Fiji. When you walk through the market on Saturday and see that stuff selling for $5 a pop, feel good. We're just saying, the small things, learn to appreciate them. Okay, maybe we are kidding . . .

THE TINSELTOWN TEST: TAKE 2

6. Which of the below is an actual living, breathing agent?
  a. William Morris
  b. Barney Greengrass
  c. Fred Segal
  d. Boaty Boatwright

7. It's your first day on the job and you're handed a pile of receipts that the last assistant conveniently forgot to expense. Which of the below should you NOT expense?
  a. The $100 Saturday brunch at the Beverly Hills Hotel with a hairstylist.
  b. The $500 champagne for the actor who just won a SAG award.
  c. The $30 Tower gift certificate for the niece's birthday.
  d. The $2,000 anniversary party dinner at Morton's that Goldie Hawn attended.

8. You've just had a stapler thrown at your head for something that wasn't your fault. You . . .
  a. duck, then quickly pick up the staples now littering the $10,000/square foot Italian marble floors.
  b. duck, then explain why you are not to blame for the mistake.
  c. duck, then walk straight out of the office knowing that you will never be able to work in this town again.
  d. don't duck, in hopes that the stapler will make contact with your face, maybe lacerate a cornea, so you can sue for damages.

9. They're serving Jerry's Deli at today's staff lunch. Your boss is a vegetarian. You . . .
  a. ask your boss if you should order something else.
  b. do nothing. If your boss gets mad you can just pretend that no one told you.
  c. call Jerry's and have them add a grilled cheese to the order.
  d. celebrate, knowing that there will probably be enough leftovers for you to take home for dinner.

10. Your boss's significant other calls but your boss twirls the busy finger. You say that your boss . . .
  a. is tied up on the other line.
  b. just went for a pee break.
  c. is in a story meeting.
  d. is nowhere to be found.

ANSWERS: 6. d; **7.** c; **8.** a; **9.** c; **10.** c

TAKE 3:
THE SHOOT

LOOK AT THAT! YOU'RE FINISHED WITH THE MINUTIAE OF PRE-production and are now ready to move on to the big shoot. Really, we knew you weren't a quitter. Well, we hoped. Now we're ready to begin the hard part.

What's that? You need a little more time to rest? Ha, that's funny. Really. Because there's no more resting allowed here. Not when you have a buttload more to learn. This next phase of your education, which we've so cleverly dubbed The Shoot, will move beyond the basics and into more treacherous territory, from dealing with celebrities to planning a dinner party to name-dropping your boss into a Lakers game. You'll gain the confidence of your boss and lay the groundwork for the idea that you will soon be ready for the next phase of your career—namely, getting promoted.

"Oh, I can practically smell it!" you rejoice.

Really, that's funny, because we were just thinking how little you can actually smell—that is, how far you are from being prepared. Seriously, being a good assistant, and thus executive, is much more than answering phones and booking some jets. We have many more lessons for you to learn before you get to that corner office, as well as some of the most important, time-tested, live-or-die-by tricks of the trade you'll need before you graduate to the next level. Believe us, we don't give these out to just anyone. Just our favorites. Which includes you, as long as you do the work.

P.S. If you pay close attention, reading between the lines and so forth, there are personal rewards in this section for you, too. And we're not just talking about taking home your boss's leftovers from Matsuhisa.

Make It About You

Boss: "So your cat died, you broke your femur, and your identity was stolen. And this affects me how?"

THERE ARE SOME THINGS ABOUT HOLLYWOOD that will never change. Skeevy older men will date slutty younger women, plastic surgeons will outnumber social workers, one's personal fortune will be worth more than one's personal relationships, and a boss will always care about one person more than anyone else: Themselves. Well, we're here to tell you that you will also have to care about one person more than anyone else: Yourself.

Refer back to the movie title of our lesson here. In the film, a young Eve gets hired to understudy a famous Broadway actress played by Bette Davis. That little minx knew that one person mattered more than anyone else: Eve. So she uses her proximity to Bette to learn, to befriend powerful people, and to steal Bette's entire identity! Okay, so Eve was a psycho. What we are saying is that if you don't look out for yourself, you could quickly lose track of why you became an assistant in the first place: to learn from your boss.

If there's anything we've learned, it's to follow in the footsteps of the successful. And what we've seen time and time again is that only the truly egomaniacal make it in the Biz. Hence, you come first, not Eve (or Kip or Theresa or whatever your boss's name is). The trick is to make your boss think that she is the only person in the room when, in actuality, you are looking out for yourself.

For instance, did your producer boss ask you to drive all the way to Tarzana on a Saturday to pick up dailies? Let's hope you used your time on the set to get to know the director. The director wouldn't even look at you? Fine, then you should have befriended his assistant. What about that time you spent three hours organizing a conference call with the actor, agent, and studio exec? Let's hope you didn't spend the entire call sending personal e-mails. No, you should have been listening to it, paying close attention to how your boss skillfully managed to dissuade the actor from dropping out of the movie. You see, these are examples of constantly educating yourself, however annoying or menial or stressful that education may be.

Don't do this and you'll end up a victim of **Stockholm syndrome,** that disturbing disorder where prisoners develop the warm-and-fuzzies for their captors. Trust us, we've seen many assistants get so obsessed with pleasing their bosses, even talking about their bosses' personal lives more than their own, that they lose all sense of themselves. That, my friends, is no way to live.

Please Don't Touch the Celebrities

"I totally never do this but, omigod! Halle Berry!! It's truly a privilege to meet you ..."

DON'T BE THAT GUY. PLEASE PLEASE, DON'T BE that guy. You know, the one who decides to walk through the lobby four times while Julia Roberts is waiting for her meeting. Or the gal who brings George Clooney his seltzer water but then proceeds to drum up a conversation about her favorite *ER* episode: "George, I have to ask you. When you were submerged in that car underwater while rescuing that kid, what was that like? I mean, did you get frostbite, or did they catch it all in one take?"

It's okay. We all have that one celeb who we dream of sharing a beer with while listening to stories about *The Facts of Life* days. When you do happen to meet such a celeb, however, take a deep breath. We simply can't have you shaming yourself. It doesn't matter where you are, who you are with, or how appropriate you think it is: You must never be a gawker. Really, nobody wants to associate with, dare we use an expletive in front of the kids, a starf#&%er.

"But they started talking to *me*," you say. Sure they did. Here's the thing: Even if a major star is waiting in your office and seems eager to chat with you, the following conversation is still not permissible:

"Thanks for the Snapple."

"Sure. I noticed you like the Diet Peach."

"Yeah."

"It reminds me of that scene in *Thelma and Louise* before you were a big star ..."

No!! Just get back to work. We promise you, befriending Brad in the waiting area isn't going to catapult your career forward. Keep your conversations professional and discreet. P.S. This extends to your mother, too, even if she is visiting all the way from Louisville and always fantasized about meeting Bobby Redford. Keep her hands off.

ON THE OTHER HAND, YOU STALKER . . .

There are, of course, times when it is okay to interact with a celeb. Rare as these are, you simply must pounce on an opportunity like the one described below:

"She was one of the most beautiful girls I'd ever seen. I mean, the entire world pretty much agreed, especially after that movie that was marketed entirely around her bikini. When I got promoted to P—'s desk, I knew she was one of his clients. She was always really friendly over the phone. She even learned my name the first time around, which, if you know anything about dealing with clients, is not normal. She'd ask me things like, 'What are you doing tonight?' or 'Did you see what Jessica Simpson was wearing at the MTV Video Awards?' After a few weeks of that she finally came in the office for a meeting. So I was at my desk, sending out some headshots for a pilot or something, when I heard someone go, 'So you're V—.' It was her, man! Standing in front of my cube!! Next thing I know we're on a friggin' date and we were vibing, man. Finishing each other's sentences, laughing about the same Simpsons episodes. It was awesome. So, no, I wasn't that surprised when she asked me out again. I know, I know, you think I'm just trying to seem cool. But really, it wasn't like that. She was just a girl, like any girl, and that's how I acted around her. Which, truth be told, is why I think we're still together."

—V. Y.

There's No Such Word as "Can't"

"Call Namibia and see if they can find the watch I lost in 1983 during my visit to the Romancing the Stone set."

IT'S 8 P.M., YOU'RE JUST SHUTTING DOWN YOUR computer and looking forward to meeting your friends for a nightcap/bitchfest when, all of a sudden, your boss calls. He wants you to send his girlfriend a dozen tulips at her parents' house in Kamloops, Canada—"Tonight!!"

First instinct: Open the Yellow Pages, flip to Assassin, and hire someone to go over to said boss's house and deliver a swift injection of formaldehyde.

Reality check: Stop freaking out. Just go online and find the number of the most expensive hotel in the area (First choice: Four Seasons. Last choice: Econo Lodge). Ask to be connected to the concierge and tell Roy, working the night shift, that your boss is a guest of the hotel. Hand over a credit card number, and let Roy run with the task (with a follow-up fax and e-mail, of course). If he calls your bluff, tell him the truth and beg him to help a brother out. Promise him that there's a *Spy Kids 2* bobblehead in it for his kids if he comes through. We promise, you'll be amazed how many people will do you a favor in return for worthless movie paraphernalia. Concierges are your best allies. Milk them for all their worth.

The answer to most requests, no matter how insane or impossible they may seem, can actually be figured out if you ask for help. Hollyweird is full of people specializing in niche fields and who are just dying for the chance to help you out.

Need to find an antique toy train for the movie star's whiney son? Call the prop house. Have to ship a pair of jeans from Milan to the actress shooting a scene in Australia 24 hours later? Midnite Express exists just for this reason. (True story from a friend by the way— $20K in shipping fees later, it was obvious why this movie was overbudget.)

Trust us, if your boss asks you to do something, never act like you don't know how. Pretend that it's no problem, make a few frantic phone calls, and make the impossible possible. Only after all else fails do you go tell the boss it can't happen. They fire you? Hell, at least you know you tried. And there is no shame in trying. Really. Even if you fail.

Befriend the Computer Geek

"My computer's broken. Totally broken! I lost everything there!"

UNLESS YOUR BOSS IS IN HIS TWENTIES AND actually had e-mail in college, he will most likely be computer illiterate. We're talking no capacity to take care of minor technological hiccups like, say, pulling up the Google homepage. In fact, it's probably the one thing that your boss and Grandma Tipsy have in common. Just as you've spent hours extracting the *Lord of the Dance* video out of the VCR after Granny put it in the wrong way, you'll need to handhold your boss when it comes to basic modern technology.

At first you might be tempted to try and teach the dog a new trick, but trust us here, don't waste your time teaching him how to save a JPEG or sync his own BlackBerry. Chances are you will spend twice as long doing it yourself after he's managed to wipe his entire address book clean.

"My Rolodex!! It just went away. I pressed a button and, pfft, it just disappeared."

"What button?"

"I don't know. Jesus, can't you just find it? I have my whole life in there."

"Sure thing, boss. I wouldn't want you losing your whole life."

How best to cope with the tech-challenged superior? Hire help. That means rather than channeling your energy into Computer 101, find a computer geek and make him your new best friend. If you don't have the wherewithal to pay him, then get creative. Schmooze your techie with swag. Send him free DVDs, regift the Starbucks card the boss got for Xmas, or offer to buy him lunch on the expense account. He will undoubtedly become one of your best allies. And since you gave him four mochaccinos and every season of *X-Files* on DVD, maybe he won't hate you so much when you call him at 7 A.M. because the network is down and your boss can't read e-mails (i.e., the battery ran out of juice).

If your boss won't let you help, do your best to keep them away from modern technology in the first place. Don't let them buy that new cell phone just because all their friends have one. Keep them in the stone age. That's what they get for expecting you to be Bill Gates.

Spend the Holidays Spending

"Rick loved that 18th-century print of his favorite region in Provence that you found. Why don't you grab him another one for Christmas?"

SURE, I'LL GO GRAB IT. BECAUSE IT ONLY TOOK me 139 man-hours to locate the first one. And while I'm at it, how about I throw in that gift basket of high-end cheese you had me get for your mistress? You know, the one that the company paid extra for so that we could messenger it to her remote winter house 73 miles due east of London?

As you would expect, in Tinseltown, the holidays have become a magical time we like to call **COC** (Christmas on Cocaine). There are the usual gift-giving sprees that the rest of the world experiences, and then there's COC: a joy ride of sin and gluttony for people who have everything, need nothing, and are so particular about everything, anyway, that they are impossible to shop for. Depending on whom you work for, you may have to purchase gifts for the boss, his family, and, if you're really unlucky, everyone in his Rolodex. We suggest the following tips to help you survive the holidays.

Christmas needs to start in November. Maybe October, if it's your first time. Plan ahead.

Make a Christmas database to save yourself the headache for the following year. Half of the work is developing the list of recipients.

Need ideas for actual gifts? Try these:

- **Wally's Liquors** (310-475-0606; www.wallywine.com) has wine and gift baskets for everyone. They'll gift wrap, messenger, and save you the hassle.

- **Kinara Spa** (www.kinaraspa.com). Everyone needs to experience at least one facial from the famous Olga at Kinara in West Hollywood, and if it's not someone's cup of tea, it's always an easy regift. Who knows, maybe the boss will throw you one of his own.

Super big extra points if you can convince the boss to look inward and give everyone the gift that keeps on giving: a card with money donated in her name to a favorite charity. Our top nine:

- **Teach For America** Aims to close the achievement gap between children of different socioeconomic backgrounds (www.teachforamerica.org)

- **Fulfillment Fund** Mentors help aspiring academics gain admission to college and win scholarships (www.fulfillment.org)
- **Los Angeles Mission** A shelter for thousands of L.A.'s homeless (http://losangelesmission.org)
- **Shoah Foundation** The Steven Spielberg-founded organization records the testimonies of Holocaust survivors (www.usc.edu/schools/college/vhi)
- **AIDS Project Los Angeles** Raises money and provides services for people living with AIDS (www.apla.org)
- **Leukemia and Lymphoma Society** Aims to cure leukemia and lymphoma, and to improve the quality of life of patients and their families (www.leukemia-lymphoma.org)
- **National Breast Cancer Foundation** Strives to save lives by increasing awareness through education and by providing mammograms to those in need (www.nationalbreastcancer.org)
- **KCRW** L.A.'s own National Public Radio station (www.kcrw.com)
- **Habitat for Humanity** Builds houses for families who otherwise couldn't afford them (www.habitat.org)

TO GIFT OR NOT TO GIFT: THE HOLIDAY DILEMMA

It's the holidays. You can barely afford to buy a Tonka for your kid brother when your coworker asks you what you're getting your boss. "What?! My boss makes like 300 percent more money than me. What the hell can I get her that she can't afford herself?" We know, it sucks. There are even some people out there who will tell you that it's not necessary to "gift up." We don't agree. If you don't get your boss a holiday gift, you'll seem unappreciative, especially when she presents you with a Barneys gift card that says, "I can't thank you enough. Really. You are doing a great job." Our advice on how to avoid dropping a bundle on a meaningless gift the boss will never use (the so-last-season pashmina you found on sale at TJ Maxx for instance): Be creative. Does your boss have a dog who she just adores? Go to kodakgallery.com and have the dog's picture printed on a set of mugs. Or better yet, just buy the dog a gift (same for the boss with kids). Did you hear him mention to a friend that it's been years since anyone's given him a toy? Buy him a remote control car to play with in the office. See, it's not the size of the gift but rather the meaning behind it.

★ *A gift for the dog is a gift for the boss.*

Recruit Your Own Intern Army

THERE ARE SOME THINGS IN HOLLYWOOD WE SIMPLY ADORE. THE open bar at premieres. The fresh fruit toppings at Pinkberry.* Meryl Streep. And then there's the large quantity of unpaid labor just ripe for the picking—yeah, interns!

In terms of improving the overall quality of your office life, there is nothing better than interns. Seriously, even if you work in an accounting firm in Dallas, you should already be taking advantage of these young tykes in need of school credit. Interns can do all the mundane things you may need in a pinch: brew coffee, run to the bookstore, and alphabetize your leaning tower of scripts. They'll also answer your phones, update your Rolodex, and temp for you while you get that rash checked out at the doctor. Better is that you don't have to give them anything in return. They exist for you, not the other way around.

Still, we're not recommending that you be mean to your interns. On the vindictive food chain that is Hollywood, they are the smelt. So when mad, try and treat them like you wish you were treated. At least you're getting paid to be demeaned.

Where to find them? The best interns are FOOIs (friends of other interns). Get the good ones who take initiative, not the apathetic ones waiting for tasks to be served up on a platter. If that doesn't work, contact the USC and UCLA career centers. Before you know it your inbox will be swamped with eager beavers salivating to pick up your— I mean your boss's—dry cleaning.

Oh, we almost forgot. Never *ever* hire the "actor" intern. You can always recognize him by the

★ *Let interns do the balancing act.*

Pinkberry frozen yogurt (www.pinkberry.com) is an alternative and far safer form of crack. Made from all natural ingredients and available in two flavors (plain and green tea—that's all, folks!), this dessert took L.A. by storm when it first appeared. Lines extend out the door at all times of the day, and they even have a velvet rope and bouncer to keep customers from fighting one another.

manila envelope full of headshots that he carries with him. He figures working here will increase his chances of being discovered by the director who thought she was coming to a professional office, not a safe haven for struggling actors.

THE ART OF THE INTERN INTERVIEW

Interviews with prospective interns should be treated more like first dates than professional interactions—meaning, you need to figure out whether you want them hanging around your cube all day. Here are some sample questions:

It's Saturday night. What are you doing?
This is a great one to figure out whether or not your future intern has an ounce of savvy or, better yet, if he is a poseur who will answer questions just so they sound good. Does he go to candlelight meditation Saturday night followed by sushi solo and a good book? Does he play online poker by himself in a dank apartment? Or is he rolling to Forty Deuces because he wants to seem cool? And if he actually is cool, will he give you attitude when you ask him to empty your recycling bin?

My boss likes her interns to have similar taste—what's your favorite movie?
Does she give you the ringers, or does she have interesting taste? "You've probably heard this before, but I just go gaga for any of the *Godfather*s." Don't hire her. You want a human after all, not a drone.

What do you want to be when you grow up?
Beware the person who claims he knows the answer to this. We're sure he doesn't. And lying that he does is a big red flag.

Are you okay with being bored?
This is a trick question. You want to make sure your intern can entertain herself. That means she can find work when you've given her none, or just keep herself busy when you're too busy to dream up tasks.

Beef Up the Rolodex

> *"I need Kevin Bacon's number ASAP. I think he's staying in that ecological park on that island chain off of Australia."*

AS A RULE, WHETHER YOU WORK AS A HOLLY-wood assistant, insurance broker, or Gap salesclerk in your hometown mall, your boss will ask you for a piece of information as soon as you have no access to it. Eleven P.M. on a Wednesday? That's when they'll want the home phone number for that agent they've never talked to before. Five A.M. on a Monday? That's when they'll berry you to say they never got that script they never asked for. Noon on a Sunday? That's when they'll be in desperate need of the Almodóvar screener they swore they'd never watch.

Sometimes you can't avoid going into the office during off-peak hours, but if you prepare well you will be able to handle most requests with a quick e-mail or phone call. Hence, get the cell number of every assistant you talk to. No, really, we're not kidding. You'll be surprised whom you'll need to track down at a moment's notice. Jamie Foxx in Miami? Check. The costume designer for the movie where the star actress is 30 kilos overweight? Check. The long lost brother who they haven't called since 1974?

"Do you want the home, cell, or yacht number??"

By using your network of fellow peons, you can call someone who will know someone who dated the assistant to the roommate of the junior agent who works with the person your boss needs to find. It's a

★ *You're nobody unless you have everybody's number.*

little time-consuming, but in a town where everyone knows everyone, you're only six degrees of separation from being able to call your boss back within an hour and casually say, "Here's Mr. Bacon's resort. They're the Whitsunday Islands, by the way. Maybe you should consider going there for a few months, and stop friggin' bothering me!" Okay, that last part stays inside your head.

YOLANDA WATSON
-star of ABC hit "ASPEN GIRLS."
Assistants Jada and Mariah are at
(j) 393-555-3344, (m) 310-555-5545

ASSTS ARE ALWAYS WITH HER,
DO NOT CALL DIRECTLY

Ron Loveliner (cute)
CAA: 310 288-4545
Assts: JANET, JANE, KATHY
CASSANDRA, JOHN, JAMIE
only call thru office
NO EXCEPTIONS

BRIAN STEINBERGER
(produced CHRISTMAS WITH PAPA)
Birthday: 7/19. Loves Vodka, First Edition
Books by Russian Authors. Cell- 310-555-3827
Deer Valley Home- No cell reception.
Call Housekeeper at 372-555-9287
Bali Home- 011 62 555 749 2629

Sage Myrtle
HAIR EXTENSIONS COLORING
RED CARPET STYLES —
cell: 917 555-7009
* DOES NOT CUT HAIR

Act Up So the Boss Will Pipe Down

"OH MY GOD! You didn't get the white truffle mustard on the side? I'll call Spago and have them fire the guy who took our order."

THIS IS ONE OF THOSE THAT WE STOLE FROM a friend and can be used in any job in any office on earth. What's the trick? The Overreaction/Underreaction System.

The secret to being a good assistant *and* staying happy is becoming a master at psychological manipulation. By deftly employing techniques such as double-talk, reverse psychology, and mental foreplay, you can be sure your boss will eventually be the putty in your hands you always dreamed he or she would be. Which brings us to the following scenario. Pay close attention:

"Boss, are you *sure* you don't want that armored car in Bosnia?"

"No armored car necessary, Kyle."

"You *sure* about that? Because I can call Music Express right now and make sure they have the best armored car to take you around Herzegovina. Bulletproof windows and all."

"That's really nice that you thought of that, but like I said, I'll be fine."

"Fine is fine, but I want you to be more than fine. I want you to be happy. And I really think you might want that sense of relief that comes from knowing you're not going to be shot. So do you want the car? Really, think twice before you say no."

"Shut up, Kyle."

You're probably confused. But Kyle, by our book, handled this situation impeccably. You see, by overreacting to a situation, he gave his boss only one option: to underreact. It's the simple rule of physics after all: Every action produces an equal and opposite reaction. Abide by this rule and you'll both protect yourself when things go wrong and simultaneously convince your boss that you are truly concerned about his welfare. Say the boss gets to Bosnia and realizes Kyle was right—he should have gotten that armored car. That leaves the boss with only one person to blame for the bullet hole in his passenger side door—himself. Nice work, Kyle!

"Hi boss, how's Bosnia?"

"Kyle, I'm scared . . ."

"Sorry . . . what? I can't hear you with the gunshots in the background, boss. Can you call me back on another line?"

Take the Truth Tonic

DON'T EVEN TRY IT, G. IT'S NOT GOING TO WORK BECAUSE YOU will be tempted. And chances are you will give in to that temptation at least several times a day. We're talking about the little white lie. Yes, you will lie on the job. To fib is human. (Just ask Catherine Zeta-Jones, age 29.) Just don't be a stupid human—admit your mistakes.

Why? Because it will come back to haunt you. And don't tell us your lies put others to shame. Believe us, we heard them all before. We can't tell you how many stories we've heard about the assistant who got fired after telling a lie that quickly blew up in her face. There's the one about the "petty cash getting donated to the Red Cross," or the meeting that the "other" assistant screwed up, or the script that "I swear I page-counted before FedExing to Joaquin." What will result is a typical Snowball of Untruths, barreling down the mountain straight for your cube. Don't wait for the avalanche.

First, other assistants will be called into the office in order to set the record straight, and all of them will sell you out the first chance they get. Second, you'll be asked to show evidence to support your claims, evidence that of course doesn't exist. Third, you'll find yourself concocting more lies so elaborate that you'll soon feel like Raskolnikov (protagonist, *Crime and Punishment,* you should know this).

We know, it's scary telling the truth, but this is one of those times when you have to look your fear in the face. That means not only telling your boss when you've mucked it up, but also telling him way before he finds out. Yes, it's critical to get ahead of the lie. Sure, he'll be mad, but even the most psycho boss will appreciate that you told him about it ahead of time. This approach also allows him to devise a way to deflect the shitstorm that may now be heading his way as a result of your screwup.

An even better alternative to the lie? Fixing the problem way ahead of time. "Hey boss, I dropped that call from Steven Spielberg yesterday. I know, I know, there's no excuse. I royally messed up. But I spoke to his assistant and explained that it was my fault. She put you on his phone sheet and promised Steven wouldn't even know."

They still fire you? That's okay. You proved yourself to be a standup guy/girl (one of few in this town), and chances are even the craziest of bosses will recognize that honesty trumps fallibility. Just make sure it doesn't happen twice.

Drop It Like It's Hot

"Do you know who I work for?"

NAME-DROPPING IN L.A. IS LIKE RHINO-plasty—when done right it will open doors ("Hi, Ashlee"); when done wrong, it can kill, or maim, a career (a certain 40-something actress once dubbed "America's Sweetheart"). You best pay attention to the following rules in order to successfully master the fine art of **the name-drop:**

1. Get over your embarrassment. You must name-drop, mister—no getting around it. "But it's so tacky. Not to mention transparent." You're right about that. Using your name to get into exclusive establishments or acquire products unavailable to the rest of the world is disgusting. But you're going to have to do it. Ten or 15 times a day, most likely.

2. No venue is out of bounds. You'll be stunned by the diversity of arenas where name-dropping works marvelously. Restaurants are a given. If you mention that your director boss is responsible for the country's number 1 comedy, a free table will mysteriously appear where there were none before. Same goes for limited-edition cars, hard-to-get airline seats, and visas to war-torn countries. What's even worse is that name-dropping even applies to hospital beds. Gasp! We know, you'll be pretty disgusted once you find out that your boss, in need of his third liver transplant this decade (thank you, Jack Daniels), has just been bumped up to the top of the donor list because he was nominated for an Oscar last year.

3. Confidence is key. So your boss's biggest credit is Associate Producer on *Ernest Goes to Camp*? Whatever. The swankiest restaurant in town need not know that. Really. Just flip to the next rule. You are going to make that hostess at Nobu believe your boss is the most important goddamn producer who ever lived.

4. Avoid the threat. There will always be that one person who won't care who the hell your boss is. "But it's Jack, Miss. *Nicholson.* He simply must have the table by the window." To which you might get, "I don't care if your boss is Jack frigging Jesus. We've got no tables available and that's that." It's at this point where you'll be tempted to invoke The Threat: "If you don't do this for me I'll tell Page Six your famous yellowtail roll from Kyoto actually hails from Rosarito!" Just kidding. Don't go there. Really. Even if you do have a friend at the *Post*.

5. Scrounge for leftovers. The only good thing about name-dropping for your boss is that you too will reap the benefits. That club with the line around the block? Call ahead and tell the owner your bigwig boss is sending you to scout out locations for a premiere. The Golden Globes bash with all the nominees? The doorman will pull back the rope once you offer him your card with the studio logo. Just don't forget the Benjamin that goes with it.

In the end, you'll turn into a name-dropping pro. Just don't let it seep into your personal life.

"I had dinner with Katie last night. Maybe you heard of her. Kate Winslet . . ."

Ew, we're so turned off right now. Really. Just flip to the next rule.

Break Out the Break

"Omigod, did you hear Madonna is running for president? I just read it on Perez."

THE NONSTOP RINGING! THE CONSTANT scheduling changes! The fiancé nagging you for the confirmation number for the Kona honeymoon! Sometimes the stress of your new job is going to take its toll on you. You fear you might crack. Hell, you've even considered jumping off the roof of your Beverly Hills office building.

This is where we come in.

Sometimes the simplest solution to a stressful moment is to take a break. Yeah, right, because your boss is totally cool with you going outside to smoke a doobie. That's not what we meant. A break in Hollywood does not entail leaving your desk but rather using your desk in new ways.

Look around you. For one, you've got Internet access. Just think of the infinite amount of reading material at your fingertips. Blogs, namely, are perfect for a mental catnap. Sure, we'd love to read *The New York Times* every day but by the time we're one sentence into the article on the universal health care bill, the boss is blowing orders into his blowhorn. Wait, you don't think monitoring the Olsen twins' eating habits is more important than the president's State of the Union address? Oh, honey bunny. You better start looking for a new job.

Two, personal errands. Pay your gas bill, check your credit card balance, or buy those shoes you found on Zappos.com. E-commerce is key if you're going to keep that wardrobe spruced up.

Three, personal calls. You say it's unethical to use the company phone to call your best friend from college who currently lives in Kyoto? Too bad, because you just logged 51 minutes discussing absolutely nothing with him. Don't lose touch with the people most important in your life. Really, that would be bad. But maybe next time turn the 51 to a more reasonable 15 minutes.

Four, better yourself. Read a book, look into weekend volunteer opportunities, or write an e-mail to your local congressman about the ozone situation.

Point is, it's imperative to slack off every once in awhile. Otherwise you will quickly become a soulless, boring, one-dimensional leech who does nothing but live for the boss. These people, by the way, are not fun to be around.

OUR FAVORITE THINGS!
THE BLOG EDITION

■ **PEREZHILTON.COM.** With trashtastic gossip and scandalous pictures to boot, Perez has brilliantly branded himself as the world's most renowned and trusted gossip columnist. Permanently situated at the Coffee Bean on Sunset, he's the first to know who's going to rehab, who's sleeping with who, and who's about to come out of the closet.

■ **DEFAMER.COM.** The Be-All and End-All of Hollywood Behind-the-Scenes Gossip. Don't be caught with your pants down—look here to find out which conglomerate is planning to lay off thousands of employees, aka you.

■ **TMZ.COM.** Gossip funded by a big conglomerate. That means the paparazzi working for this site actually get paid disgusting amounts to get not only pictures but *live video* of drunk celebs crashing their cars, attacking people on the street, and saying things that no sober person would ever say.

■ **GOFUGYOURSELF.COM.** Photos of the worst-dressed celebs, updated daily.

■ **GAWKER.COM.** For when you're feeling more intellectual. Who are we kidding? It's just gossip that's more N.Y. than L.A.

■ **PINKISTHENEWBLOG.COM.** Perez's top competitor, Trent offers kinder, gentler gossip. No wonder he's not as successful. Still, we like the bubble letters.

■ **FLESHBOT.COM.** NO NO NO. You can't be looking at this stuff at work.

■ **EONLINE.COM.** When times are REALLY tough. Straight to the fashion police.

Fight the Power

SOMETIMES YOU'LL HAVE TO TAKE ONE FOR THE TEAM. FOR example, there was that time you came up with the idea to put Johnny Depp in *Pirates of the Caribbean* and your boss took the credit. Or when you were told to do notes on four scripts the one night Mom and Dad were visiting and no one even bothered to discuss them in the development meeting. Or how about that time you stood up in the board meeting and told the entire staff it was your fault your boss wasn't there, even as you knew he was just tied up in a colonic?

The nature of any job is to be your boss's doormat, and chances are she'll wipe her shoes on you whenever she wants. However, there is only so much abuse you should take. After that you must raise arms and fight back. There is no assistant union, so here are some questions to ask yourself to figure out how to pick your battles:

- **Could sticking up for yourself truly advance your career?** For example, are you not allowed to leave your desk for lunch, resulting in a cranky outlook and a really fat ass? Well, we agree, that does sound like it sucks, but demanding a free hour a day for lunch certainly won't make you a C.E.

- **Are you willing to lose your job over it?** In other words, is this issue more important than your paycheck? We're talking moral conflict, ethical dilemma, or a damaged reputation. Notice we did not say pride. If you can walk out that door with your head held high, then go for it. If you're going to regret it a week later, bite that tongue.

- **Do you have backup proof?** If you're claiming that you deserve credit for something that you haven't been given credit for, you better be able to provide evidence.

- **If you were allowed only one battle the entire year, would this be it?** Pick wisely. Only after weighing your options should you pick up the proverbial picket sign. Try to have some back-up, though. One assistant out sick won't make a dent. But an entire office of asistants? Think of the chaos! Remember, what hurt you today may be a distant memory tomorrow. Make sure it's really worth it.

- **Do you have a Plan B?** So you stood up for yourself and it backfired. Do you have another job lined up? Contacts that will still be willing to help you out? Think twice if your answer is no.

BATTLE FIGHTERS:
TRUE STORIES FROM THE TRENCHES

Whether you're trying to be Bill Murray, Bill Clinton, or Bill Gates, here are some real-life stories from assistants who knew when to fight the good fight.

Anne read a major spec script and thought it was brilliant. She berried the boss at 11 P.M. to tell her to read immediately. Studio buys it the next morning and packages it ASAP. Good work, Anne. Now if only you knew how she got credit where credit was due. "How?!" you pant. By letting it be known to everyone in the hall (execs, assistants, the janitor) that it was she who read it first. She didn't brag, but rather slid it into conversation. Oh, and lookee there, Anne even had the e-mail as proof, the same e-mail she bcc'ed all the junior-level executives on when she originally sent it. KUTGW,* Anne!

Lewis told his boss about a cult comic book he found in his grandfather's attic. Cut to three years later and the film version is outgrossing *Batman* at the box office. Good thing Lewis demanded an associate producer credit (even if he didn't have any real involvement). You see, Lewis knew that good ideas are rare. If he didn't make a name for himself this time around, he might not have another chance for 20 years.

The assistants at X Production Company worked 20 hours of overtime a week but didn't get paid for it. Guess what? Join the club. Here's what was *not* okay: They also didn't get paid vacations. So one enterprising assistant rallied the others and together they went to the head of H.R., formally asking for either paid overtime or paid vacation. After all, these work practices are against the law. "You don't want the Better Business Bureau to find out about it, right?" Two weeks later they were all getting two weeks vacation paid and signed for by X.

Juan-Carlo read every script that came through his high-powered boss's office, but his boss was so oblivious that he didn't know Juan-Carlo's last name, let alone his amazing story sense. Rather than stew about it, Juan-Carlo let the more junior level execs know about all the extra hard work he was doing. Then when a C.E. job opened up, the junior execs were quick to recommend Juan-Carlo for the job. You know how the Big Boss responded? "Who's Juan-Carlo?" Still, Juan-Carlo ended up getting the gig.

Keep up the good work.

Love Your Boss's Love

"Do you mind coming over to the house tonight and wallpapering the nursery? Maybe pick up some pad thai on your way, too. I'm totally swamped."

AH, YES, DEALING WITH THE **S.O.** (SIGNIFICANT other). The one. Yoga teacher, Barneys salesgirl, or, Beelzebub herself, an actress.

They're all the same, really. They're in love with your boss (more likely his money) and have way too much time on their hands. It's the reason they're calling you up every five minutes to make last-minute reservations at Asia de Cuba or find that rehydrating facial elixir that he bought her on their weekend getaway to Paris.

Chances are you will grow to dread this person. No matter how nice, sweet, or attractive she is, you will not be able to get past the fact that she represents one thing and one thing only for you—more work. You might want to scream, "I work for your spouse, not you! Pick the heinie off the couch and do it yourself!"

And you'd be right. The corporate office would not look kindly on the fact that your work productivity is drastically decreasing because you're swamped ordering pink Post-it notes for the home office. Or that you are FedExing clothes from Baby Gap to the significant other's sister in London. But they're not going to find out. Why? Because you will do every single thing the S.O. asks, and like it.

"Seriously??"

Seriously. There's no better way to sabotage your job than pit your boss's S.O. against you. Nod happily, use phrases like "I'll get right on it," and act like you love the lime green blouse she's wearing. It'll be hard to swallow, but you'll be glad you did it. Especially when your birthday rolls around and she's the one picking out your gift. Lord knows you need another bloody Starbucks card. Your closet could really use that pair of Prada shoes about now.

There is, of course, the S.O. who you will love—and befriend. After all, you are the two people in the world who knows your boss best. Enjoy the lovefest. Bond over your boss's annoying tics. Commiserate about his bad temper. Laugh about his odd fashion sense. Both you and the S.O. know the guy needs to be taken down a notch every now and then.

THE MANY FACES OF A SIGNIFICANT OTHER:

CRAZED CAROL: Just as crazy busy as your boss. Has no time to do anything, and thus is constantly overbooked, overwrought, and overly annoying. Leaves you cryptic messages that you can't understand on voicemail. "Friday. Dinner. The Andersons. Are they on Atkins still? Tell Brandy. Brandy is chef, no more Christo." It takes so much time to decipher what she needs from her disorganized life, you *almost* wish she were a bit more like . . .

LARRY THE LOST: This one can really throw you for a loop. He doesn't actually do anything for a living, but wants to do *everything*. Classes on the Middle East. Poker parties. Scuba diving certification. With more hobbies than time, he has constant pesky questions like . . . "I hear there's a new ashram in the Valley? Is this true? Whatever came of that restaurant Wolfgang was opening? Can you make reservations there? What's a reduction sauce?" At least you don't have your coworker's spouse, otherwise known as . . .

SUZY SPA: From what you can tell, the only thing that happens on a daily basis for this spouse is the spa visit. Spa-ing is like work, and she cannot miss it. When you ask her to come into the office at two for an important meeting with the hubby, she replies, "Two? Did you say two? I can't possibly get there by two. I have my blackhead purifier appointment until 1:50." You dig deep within yourself before blathering, "Why don't you get those blackheads expunged tomorrow?" or "What else is on your to-do list? Coffee Bean stop? Bang trim? Make list for personal shopper? Try to finish one bloody sudoku?"

Suck Up to the Satan Spawn

Boss:
"Reschedule my
lunch with
Jimmy."
You:
"Jimmy who?"
Boss:
"Jimmy Jimmy.
My son Jimmy.
Are you doing
drugs?"

HOLLYWOOD TYPES WORK CRAZY-ASS HOURS. Everyone knows that. However, that doesn't stop them from taking the time to procreate like the rest of this hump-happy nation. What often results is that wonderful miracle of life called a baby. Yes, the same baby your boss then proceeds to hand off to the full-time nanny. Who has time for parenting when you've got *Rambo: The Early Years* to put together, let alone that weekly manicure appointment with Gong? Priorities, people, priorities!

"But," you whine, "I came to L.A. exactly so I could escape those awful Henderson twins and their runny stool." Well, isn't that great. Because those babysitting skills are sure to come in way handy now that you're an FHPP. Hence, say hello to your new bosom buddy: the nanny.

Whether you're coordinating playdates with the A-list director's progeny, ordering diapers in bulk, or calling last minute to inform her that she will need to fill in on the mommy half of mommy-and-me, chances are your two jobs will intersect more than you'd like. And then, of course, will come the office visit, where nanny and company come dragging their saggy diapers into your cubicle. For the love of god, will it ever end?? No.

How to survive the drop-by? Keep toys handy. Candy is your new currency. Consider what a perfect changing table the photocopier is. Point is, roll up your sleeves, get down on the floor, and pretend like you're a kid again. If you follow our advice, the kids will start to talk highly of you at the dinner table, the nanny will love you for giving her a breather, and the boss will think you're the man for being able to hang with her kids. Did somebody say promotion?

TOP FIVE FUN THINGS YOU SHOULD HAVE IN YOUR OFFICE TO MAKE YOU LOOK LIKE MARY POPPINS WITH THE BOSS:

1. **Quality children's films:** The classics, not just *Cars* and *Toy Story*, but a little *Bedknobs and Broomsticks* or *The Wizard of Oz*. It makes you look smart.

2. **Games:** Candyland. Enough said.

3. **Puzzles:** Puzzles take us back to the days of old, before kids just played games online. You can tell your boss about the link between young geniuses and puzzles. Another point for you.

4. **Fluids:** Order those little juice boxes packed with natural fruit juice. The kid gets the necessary sugar high, and you'll look really on your game by proffering an alternative to soda pop for the young cub.

5. **Magic:** Study up on Houdini. Do a few card tricks. Learn how to pick a coin out of an ear. You've been pulling rabbits out of a hat for your boss all along, so pulling one out for little Brittany shouldn't be a problem.

"Abusing the messenger service is standard in this town. Bosses will have you order a messenger to pick up everything from that last bottle of White Pearl nail polish at Sephora to their biweekly stash of medicinal marijuana. Well, it gets worse. I was working for this agent. He and his wife were trying to have a baby, unsuccessfully, for years. And even though they tried to keep it a secret, everyone in the office knew who to blame; my boss's swim-team was in need of some serious endurance training, so to speak. One day he came to my desk with a small box. 'Can you messenger this package to this address right away? It's urgent.'

'Done and done,' I said and smiled back. Twenty minutes later, the package on its way to Beverly Hills, I got this call from Eli in the mailroom. There had been an 'accident.' The package was leaking a fluid, and the driver, some out-of-work screen-writer, was threatening to sue the agency if, and I quote, 'this liquid is what I think it is.' Well, that messenger was no schmo. The address my boss had given was for a doctor who runs ads in *Variety,* touting himself as 'the fertility expert to the stars' Yeah, pretty friggin' sick. Long story short, the agency agreed to rep the messenger for a year in order to prevent a lawsuit. And he actually ended up selling some action spec. Now he sits by his pool in Malibu all day, selling one-line pitches over the phone. My boss and his wife adopted a child from Ethiopia. Happy ending, I'd say." **—J.U.**

TRUE CONFESSIONS

You're Not Curing Cancer

"Randy? Yes, I know you're at your sister's wedding. But do you know where I am? Standing on a tarmac in Telluride with no jet. NO JET. Am I to take the bus back to L.A.? Agency partners don't do buses, Randy."

WHEN A JOB NIGHTMARE OCCURS, AND IT probably will, take a deep breath and say the following statement ten times:

"I'm not curing cancer, I'm just working in the movie business. I'm not curing cancer, I'm just working in the movie business. I'm not curing cancer, I'm . . ." You get the idea. (FYI: This chant works in all job fields. Except the field of cancer-curing medicine. Thanks for that, by the way.)

When things go wrong, and they will, it is vital that you keep things in perspective. Regardless of how giant your mistake, at the end of the day, it's just a mistake. The reality, of course, is that your boss will make it feel like the End of Days. Here's how not to make it worse:

- **Shut your mouth.** When the boss needs to vent (i.e., verbally abuse you), let him. Go to your happy place and then take it all in. Breathe deeply. Look humbled. Breathe deeply again. Talking back and making excuses will only piss him off even more.

- **Feign action.** Dodge the proverbial poo hitting the fan by pretending like you're already fixing the problem, even if this is the first time you've heard of it. Say things like "I'm onto it," "The car is almost there," or "I'm on hold with the airline."

- **Go doggy style.** Put on your best puppy-dog face, walk with your tail between your legs, and mope around the office. Just make it seem like you feel really bad about your screwup. Man, you make forlorn look so good.

- **Nose, meet grindstone.** Show up early and leave late the entire following week, work extra hard, triple-check all tasks, and make sure jets are on the tarmac at the appropriate time.

At the end of the day, remember, it's just a job. One from which you *may* get fired. That's just a reality you will have to accept. But it's okay. Really. As we all know, the key to life is falling down and getting back up again. And again. And again . . .

THINGS TO DO WHEN YOU GET FIRED:

The worst mistake any newly (and unwillingly) unemployed person can make is to do *nothing*. Get up, put on your best outfit, and explore.

LEARN IT: Sign up for a night class. Intro to Photography, History of Japan, or Tips for the Smart Investor. What better way to keep your brain fresh and possibly meet other like-minded people (and potential employers) than by enriching your intellect.

WRITE IT: Everyone else is doing it, so you might as well write a screenplay too. If it sucks, then you've simply joined the ranks of other wannabe writers moping across town. If it's good, and you're lucky, you're rolling around in money and a new career.

GIVE IT: Volunteering is about as good for the soul as any church outing we've ever encountered. Tutor kids, clean up the beach, or campaign for your favorite underdog politician.

HIKE IT: Choose a trail, grab a buddy, and head up the mountain to your favorite canyon. At the vista, you can view the city's enormous potential that's just waiting for you to pounce on.

ROAD TRIP IT: Vegas is three hours away, San Francisco is six, the Grand Canyon eight. Jump in the car and see where the day takes you.

"It was right after the holiday break. I had gone to Amsterdam for New Years and after partying for seven days straight came home sick as a dog. Still, we had just come back from a two-week break. I wasn't about to call in sick. So I dragged my fluey ass into the office. I figured I'd be fine. But then I had this little screwup, like I forgot to cancel her lunch and the other person was waiting for her at Mr. Chow for a half hour or something. I apologized profusely to the lunch date, telling him it was my fault, and my boss was laughing about it by the end of the day. She didn't like him, anyway. But the next day I forgot to add the CEO to the phone sheet. And then, that same night, I forgot to tell her this script called [bleep] came into the office. You know, that movie that won Best Picture and Screenplay? I was already packing my desk by the time she came in the next morning. No matter how sick I was or whatever excuse I could come up with, it didn't matter. I'd made three pretty giant mistakes in less than 48 hours. I deserved to be canned."

TRUE CONFESSIONS

—**C.T.**

Cutting Class Never Goes Out of Style

> *"Come on, dude, I'm only in town for a day. It's not like you run the joint. Why don't you take the day off?"*

YOU KNOW YOU CAN'T TAKE THE DAY OFF. If you do, who will draft that morning meeting agenda, make those Polo Lounge reservations, or fluff the boss's hemorrhoid pillow? And then there's the disaster area that doubles as your workstation—binder clips cluttering the desktop, sushi menus exploding out of file folders, and private Post-its from the guy down the hall tacked to your keyboard. What to do?

TAKE THE DAMN DAY OFF

Taking a day off will do wonders for your peace of mind. Like a power nap, it will have you returning to work rejuvenated. Even better, you'll remember that life goes on outside the hallowed halls of Hollywood. Roll down Beverly Drive at noon on a Tuesday and you'll see what we mean: People are living! Now figuring out *how* to play hooky, that's the tough part. Here's our advice:

1. **Don't ask, tell.** No one is going to take care of you if you don't take care of yourself. So don't cancel that dentist appointment for the fifteenth time and then find yourself having an emergency root canal. Tell your boss, don't ask, when you have to do small things like, I don't know, get a pap smear. If they say no, then resort to the following . . .

2. **Pull a sick one.** So your best friend has a 12-hour layover at LAX on the way home from a two-year tour of duty in the Peace Corps and you're calling in sick. We recommend anything contagious—the flu, shingles, pink eye. We love using vertigo as an excuse. You can't drive with that one. Just don't do the food-poisoning thing. It reeks of bull crap.

3. **Embarrass yourself.** There are certain excuses that your boss won't question simply because you'd have to be crazy to create a lie that humiliating. Well, guess what, you're just that crazy. What we're talking about here are things like, "I have to go to court for public indecency charges," "My younger sister needs me to accompany her to Planned Parenthood," or "I've had a flare up . . . down there."

4. Be prepared. You've known for weeks that you're taking this Wednesday off to get a full body treatment (salt scrub, chemical peel, Brazilian wax) at that cheap spa in Koreatown. Good thing the boss thinks you're driving to Reno to celebrate your grandma's 80th. Not to mention that you've left the office in impeccable shape. You see, you must prepare for being out of the office ahead of time. Have task lists, check them twice, and make certain you wrap up any loose ends. (You know, like having cast lists in the file labeled "Cast Lists.")

5. Tack up your cheat sheet. The saving grace for any assistant is having a how-to-do-my-job guide. Prepare this your first month on the job with things like: How to answer the phone. Where to order out for lunch. Who the important callers are. Make it so specific that even a monkey could figure out how to do your job for the day.

P.S. Another benefit of skipping out every once in a while is that it causes your boss to appreciate you. Bosses take their assistants for granted, and there's no better way to give one a wake-up call than by taking off a day to drink martinis poolside! (But not where the boss can find you. Best to roll it down to the O.C., where you are certain to see no one you know.)

"My mom was in town for a few days, but I wasn't planning on taking the day off. I live in Santa Monica, so I figured she could just walk to the beach and bum around the promenade all day. But then it happened. Those three days out of the entire year and right when my mom was here, it rained! I didn't want my mom to be stuck in my sty of an apartment all day (or to find my porn collection), so I asked my boss if I could take the day off to drive her around. Big mistake.

TRUE CONFESSIONS

Big mistake. Not only did I get a lecture on poor planning, but I was also accused of 'trying to sabotage the company.' You know, because the entire office would blow up and my boss's career would tank if I wasn't there for a day. The outcome? I went to work and Mom sat on the couch reading my old *Sports Illustrated*s until she got bored and started cleaning my room and found . . . yeah, I don't really want to talk about it. Next time I'm just going to call in sick." **—F.F.**

Make Sure Temps Don't Become Permanent

"Don't worry, boss. You won't even notice I'm gone."

AS IF TAKING THE DAY OFF ISN'T TRICKY enough, there's also the issue of finding someone to sit in for you. Now pay close attention here, because there is a fine art to finding the perfect temp. On one hand, you want someone smart and capable so the boss isn't calling you every five minutes while you're at your "nephew's bar mitzvah." On the other hand, you don't want this temp to be too good. Take the story of Bonnie, for instance:

Bonnie was working for an HPP when her boyfriend convinced her it was time to elope. So with only a week to plan a Vegas wedding and honeymoon, Bonnie went on the prowl for a temp. First she called up her **FBJs** (Friends Between Jobs). Because these folks were highly trained and, hence, sought after, none was available for at least a year. Next Bonnie called the temp office. Big mistake. The temp office, having no idea just how demanding Bonnie's desk was, sent over applicants unqualified to temp at Hardee's, let alone the desk of an HPP. Bonnie went into panic mode, asking everyone up and down the hall for help. Finally she got a recommendation: Melinda had recently moved here from New York, where she worked as an assistant in publishing. No, Melinda didn't know who was who in Hollywood, but she was college educated and had good phone manners. So Bonnie booked Melinda and jetted off to her wedding at the same drive-through chapel Britney Spears used.

And here, my friends, is where the story takes a turn for the worse. Melinda, no spring chicken, wasn't only smart, well put together, and polite on the phone—she was also ruthless. Seizing upon the opportunity, Miss Manipulator took every opportunity to charm Bonnie's boss as well as drop subtle comments about her "messy desk, outdated phone sheet, and inefficient filing system." Well, wouldn't you know it? Bonnie, glowing after the most romantic week of her life, arrived back to her cube to find, not a wedding gift, but Melinda now sitting at her desk . . . for good. Or as the boss put it, "Bonnie, say hello to my new assistant. Even her cappuccinos are better than yours."

How could Bonnie have avoided said tragedy? Easy.

- First, as any self-respecting assistant will tell you, have several reliable temps lined up ahead of time. Otherwise you'll never be able to take a spontaneous day off without worrying the whole time about what havoc said schmuck is wreaking on your desk. Where to find them? Look back to lesson 3 to see our favorite temp agencies.

- Second, never ever hire a temp you do not know firsthand; otherwise you risk feeling like you ended up in *Single White Female*.

- Third, set traps. Just in case your temp happens to be a better assistant than you, make it impossible for her to do your job as well. Sabotage her by, say, forgetting to tell her your boss hates to be called by his first name. Or making her wear a suit when your boss demands you wear jeans and T-shirts. But set no traps that can be traced back to you.

BONUS TIDBIT: ANOTHER WAY TO MILK YOUR INTERNS FOR EVERY LAST DROP!

Training your intern as a temp is a genius move. First, an intern will most likely still be in school and thus unable to replace you. Second, interns are notoriously green. So while more than able to complete the basics tasks, they'll have no idea what it means to go above and beyond in order to make your boss happy. After all, only you know everyone who calls in, can predict their snack cravings, or understand their gesticulations that double as orders (i.e., a twirling index finger means "call back"). Last but not least, most bosses prefer to have a temp they know and trust rather than some schmo off the street.

TRUE CONFESSIONS

"The temp I normally used canceled on me at the last minute and this guy Martin came highly recommended. So I booked him, took the day off as planned, and didn't get one phone call from the office all day. Great, right? Well, on the following Monday I'm at my desk, catching up on all the work that had piled up, and I get this phone call from an assistant at CAA. 'Lyle, what the hell? You never sent that script.' I apologized, explaining that I was out and it must have been my temp, these things happen, no big deal, yada yada. 'Lyle, what are you talking about? We I.M.'ed all day and then we talked like three times. I even asked you how your girlfriend was. Dude, are you okay?' Um, yeah, so I guess this Martin guy had signed on as my screenname, and also spent the whole day passing himself off as me over the phone. Martin never temped in our office again." —**L.H.**

THE TINSELTOWN TEST: TAKE 3

11. Your boss is on retreat for the day. Put these tasks in priority order (1 being the most important, 5 the least):

   a. Do expenses.

   b. Answer phones.

   c. Schedule meetings.

   d. Call your mom and wish her a happy birthday.

   e. Watch old screen tests and eat popcorn.

12. Julia Roberts is sitting three feet from your desk while she waits to meet with your boss. You . . .

   a. tell her *Steel Magnolias* is your favorite movie.

   b. instant message all of your friends that Julia is sitting three feet away from you.

   c. small-talk about the cheating couple on the cover of the *US Weekly* she's reading.

   d. appear extremely busy.

13. It's Saturday and you're at brunch with friends when your boss calls your cell phone. You . . .

   a. excuse yourself and go see what the boss needs.

   b. answer the phone on speaker so the friends can witness firsthand the insanity that you deal with.

   c. listen to the voicemail later.

   d. throw your phone in the closest body of water.

14. Your best friend from college is getting married in a month and you need to take two days off in order to make the Thursday night booze cruise. You . . .

   a. ask for the days off, explaining to your boss why it's important that you need to be there.

   b. ask for the days off, but say that it's your sister's wedding.

   c. call in sick from the cab on the way to the airport.

   d. skip the wedding. Work is important to you after all.

15. You think you may lose your job unless you come up with a good excuse for why you forgot your boss had $2,000 floor seats to the Lakers game (thus causing him to miss the best game of the decade). You . . .

   a. admit you made a mistake, apologizing profusely.

   b. say the tickets were stolen out of your desk.

   c. blame the computer guy who fixed your calendar but accidentally deleted the "Lakers Game" entry.

   d. laugh it off and start looking for a new job.

ANSWERS: 11. b d e c a; **12.** d; **13.** c; **14.** b; **15.** a

TAKE 4:
THE RELEASE

WOOOOOOOOOHOOOOOOOO! YOU'VE MADE IT PRETTY FAR. PAST THE midpoint even. You are to be congratulated for your hard work and dedication, young pup. It won't be long until we're sending you off to the big time, weepy-eyed as we watch you collect your Oscar statuette. But first, we push on, teaching you everything you'll need to know to enter the next phase of your career. Namely, your star-studded, red carpet, $1 million extravaganza at the Chinese Theatre otherwise known as THE RELEASE.

In this section, we show you how to start moving up the ladder. After all, our goal for you is a promotion. That means no more answering phones, no more doing expenses, no more dodging bagels. Yeehaaaaw!

At the heart of these lessons will be two things we've only hinted at until this point: image and perception. So much of what happens in this town revolves around what others perceive as true. That includes who's the next Jack Nicholson (Matt Damon), the next Spielberg (Steven Soderbergh), or the next Jodie Foster (Dakota Fanning). Without other people perceiving you as the next Studio Head, A-list Producer, Power Broker, etc., etc., and thus carrying you to the top of the Hollywood Heap, you'll be stuck exactly where you are now: the bottom.

"How can I control other people's perception of me?" you ask. "God only graced me with so many positives. What happens after that is up to fate."

Au contraire, Claire. Do you think that's what Oprah said? It's what you do with your god-given talents that will make or break your career in Hollywood. Sitting back and waiting for your destiny to happen is about as smart as marrying Tom Cruise to help your career. In other words, it doesn't work. What does is networking. Creating an image for yourself that screams FHPP involves lots and lots of schmoozing. After all, if you're not hanging out with the right people, presenting the right attitude in staff meetings, or looking right for your part, you're bound to end up being an assistant forever.

"The horror, the horror!!"

Chill. Follow our lead and you'll soon be gracing the cover of the *Hollywood Reporter*'s "Next Generation" issue.

Embrace the Bling

"My favorite book? Right, like I can afford to read when my waxing bill alone maxes out the AmEx."

STUPID, AGGRESSIVE PEOPLE GET AHEAD IN Hollywood. We know how much this sucks. You left Jersey precisely because you were sick of how Casey Poppington and her big boobs stole every Student Council election and bad boy you ever campaigned for. You came to Hollywood because you actually thought that, finally, you'd be able to escape your physical shortcomings and get ahead by working hard and exhibiting your superior intelligence. Sorry, young pup, but even in Hollywood— whom are we kidding?—*especially* in Hollywood, boobs trump brains.

"I want to be a producer, though! What do my boobs have to do with it?"

A lot. You've chosen a business that is, sorry to say so, shallow. Besides Scientology, image is the most popular religion around here. Movie stars often become movie stars not because they trained at Juilliard, but because they look like Demi Moore. A movie's success is judged by box office, not by its review in *The New Yorker*. Agents score good clients not on their strength of character but because they snagged one of the last remaining limited-edition diamond-encrusted Escalades left in North America. ("If they can buy that car, then they can definitely get the studio to pay for my double-wide trailer"—that's how actors think here.) In many ways, your own success will also depend on the image you project. Dress like a slob and you might as well tattoo "I have low self-esteem" on your forehead. Drive a jalopy and people will be embarrassed to stand next to you at the valet. Talk with your mouth full at the Ivy and, well, good luck.

We're just as appalled by this superficial Hollywood crap as you. Hell, there are times when we thought of chucking it all and moving back home to become a gym teacher, and then it hit us. We love this superficial Hollywood crap! And apparently, so does the rest of the country. Why else is Paris Hilton famous if not for everyone's desire to see *Star*'s groundbreaking report about how much she dropped on Rodeo last weekend. And come on, just because we like to read about other people being shallow doesn't mean *we* are shallow. Yes, we're saying you can go to Hollywood without *going* Hollywood.

For example, rumor has it that a certain A-list director still drives his 1992 Honda Civic. One of the town's top studio execs supposedly wore the same pair of dirty jeans 28 days straight. And then there's the one about the fabulously famous movie star who refuses to use deodorant for fear of clogging his chi with preservatives. What do all of these people have that you don't? Well, money for one, but, more important, success. That's right, they've earned the right to be slobs. Until this time comes for you, we're sorry, but you're going to have to continue looking like you spent the $500 a pop Fabrizio charges to cut your hair (even though it's your neighbor-the-beauty-school-dropout Dawn who did it for a six-pack of Corona). Don't like it? Then pack up your hairspray, go back to Jersey, and apply for a job at Hooters. We hear Casey Poppington's the manager.

Fake It Till You Make It

"What I lack in height I make up for in ego."

LOOK AROUND. DO YOU SEE THEM? NO, LOOK down. Yeah, there, closer to the ground. You see them now, right? Isn't it crazy? We totally agree. There are just so many short men in this town.

If we had to guess we'd say that there are more Napoléon complexes running around L.A. than chicks with implants. I mean, what other business is built entirely on people pretending to be something they're not? For these little fellows (check out those lifts on his shoes, by the way), shortness is just another thing to feed that insatiable ambition. No wonder they've gotten so far in the world.

Well, listen up, all you insecure people out there, because you too can get far in Dwarfwood. How do you do it? Easy. It's confidence. And you can't have enough of it. Having faith in yourself is crucial to surviving in every facet of this business; therefore, the minute you walk through the door of any office, boardroom, or hip-happening club, it is an absolute must that you exude supreme levels of confidence. Show even the slightest hint of low self-esteem and you'll be laughed back all the way to your cube.

"But what happens," you whisper, "if I really do have bad self-esteem??"

Oy. You're really going to make this difficult on us, aren't you? Our gut reaction to this question would be to leave town immediately. But we understand. Not everyone is blessed with the extraordinary gift of a large ego. So our next bit of advice would be to do what virtually everyone does: Pretend that you are confident.

Really, no one on Sunset Boulevard—or Wall Street and Capitol Hill for that matter—is as happy with himself as he pretends. It's common understanding that 90 percent of people here will lie to you about (1) their personal worth, (2) their degree of power, and (3) their sexual prowess. "That's so lame!" And we agree with you there, but a good self-esteem, and a successful Hollywood career, requires just a bit of hyperbole.

Perception is one of Hollywood's favorite words. Embrace it and allow yourself to ooze with confidence. Pretty soon, your very own assistant will be marveling at your fantastic sense of self. You won't tell her it's all an act, though. Egomaniacs never do.

OUR FAVORITE READING MATERIALS TO HELP YOU FIND THAT "I'M THE NEXT HEAD OF THE STUDIO" ATTITUDE:

- **The Power of Now,** by Eckhart Tolle. If not today, when?

- **The Alchemist,** by Paul Coehlo. Fall down seven times, get up eight! Point is, believe in the dream.

- **Civil Action,** by Jonathan Harr. It's a little lengthy, yes, but if John Travolta can play the guy who brought these peeps to justice, shouldn't you be able to procure the elusive C.E. job?

- **Blink,** by Malcolm Gladwell. Learn how to trust your instincts. No HPPs question their decisions, and neither should you.

- **O Magazine.** May we then refer you to God herself: Oprah. This woman can do anything, so you can do *one* thing and read the spiritual pep talks in this rag. (Skip to the back for the "What I know for sure . . ." essay. A straight boost to the esteem straight from Oprah's mouth.)

And if all this reading is making you tired, we recommend throwing a little "Eye of the Tiger" on your iPod. You'll be feeling ego-tastic in no time.

Get on Track

"My tracking board says Wilson is getting the boot and Keppler is leaving CAA to take over marketing. There goes the studio."

COMMUNICATION IS KEY TO SURVIVING IN Talkytown. If you're out of the loop you might as well go back to that job whippin' up shakes at Johnny Rockets. The most important form of communication in the Biz: **tracking boards.** These e-mail chain/chat rooms are the basis of every piece of information traded in Hollywood. Industryites discuss the hottest specs going out, the most coveted jobs available, and the suckers who are about to get fired. In other words, they're a contemporary version of your grandma's quilting bee. Just with cussing.

As an assistant and wannabe exec, it's your job to get on as many tracking boards as you can. "One isn't enough??" No. "How about two?" Hell, eight isn't enough. Because the more tracking boards you frequent the more information will pass your way. As we all know, information is money in this town and—last time we checked—you're broke.

HOW TO BECOME A TRACKING BOARD SLUT!

■ **Friends.** Yes, you have to be invited on a tracking board, which means you're going to have to rely on friends and FOFs once again.

■ **Always say yes.** Accept all invitations to tracking boards. You never know which will contain *the* info needed to impress the boss.

■ **Make sure to go to your tracking board drinks.** Chances are you won't want to, but the minute the others in the group sense that they're not your number one board is the same minute you'll be excommunicated.

■ **Start your own.** You'll prove yourself as a leader as well as get the chance to play dictator. Popular host websites: IFilmPro.com and Yahoo! Groups. Handed to you on a silver platter, lazybones.

Now there is something to be wary of when it comes to tracking: over-sharing. This would involve leaking the juicy tidbit that happens to sink your entire company and, oh looky there, can be traced back to you. The solution: Trade prior-traded information. Say you need to get some dirt from a tracking buddy but you need to give him some in return. Rather than divulging your own company's secret, divulge one from a competing company, a secret that you just happened to get off of one of your ten other tracking boards. You sly fox, you.

Make Love, Not War

WE ARE NOW AT THE PART IN YOUR JOURNEY TO THE CORNER Office when we want to direct your attention to the most complex and least studied of showbiz species: your fellow assistants. As you've probably figured out by now, assistants can be a rough lot. And really, who can blame them? What type of person tries to make it in an industry notorious for backstabbing, public ridicule, and corporate bloodshed? Only the most ambitious and cutthroat specimens that roam this bountiful earth. Animals, we tell you, that's what you all are.

"Not me! I'm nice. Just ask Shana, who sits in the cube next to me. Sometimes I even bring her a latte in the morning."

That's so funny, because Shana's the one who told us you spread that rumor about her sleeping with her boss—*and* her boss's wife! That was So (Not) Nice. The worst part? You have committed a cardinal sin of our Assistant Bible. You instigated a fight with a peer.

Let us explain. This industry naturally breeds conflict. Agents fight with the studio execs, who fight with the producers, who fight with the directors, who fight with the actors, who fight with their spouses, who fight with the maid. (Don't even get us started on the paparazzi.) Sounds exhausting, right? Right. Our rule: Never fight your own kind.

We can't tell you how many times we've been going about our day, trying to keep a positive attitude despite the fact that the expenses are backlogged eight months, when a fellow assistant will call up and ruin our good mood. "You didn't get my boss a drive-on!" or "You sent a script that is missing page 69. I'm telling my boss that was your fault."

Relax, people! So we made a mistake. Big whoop. We're guessing that you've probably made some, too. So rather than get all uppity, why don't you try a different approach with your fellow warriors? For example: "Hey, want to hear a funny story? My boss didn't have a **drive-on** and he just screamed at your security guard for ten minutes. Can I thank you for the pure entertainment value you just provided me?" Or "So there's a page missing from my script which, out of all pages, is page 69. Get it? Huh huh. 69. Wanna fax that puppy over?"

One approach just perpetuates the pain and suffering that your bosses inflict on you every day. The other stops the cycle of abuse, which then allows you and your fellow colleagues to bond over the ludicrous nature of your job. After all, this isn't a war you're fighting right now. It's the entertainment industry. Yes, *entertainment*. So look at your peers as potential friends, not enemies, all fighting for one common cause. What's that? To get through the day without crying. Do that and we will give you the Assistant of the Year award.

Beware the Overshare

"And then he walked out of her office with his fly unzipped. But you didn't hear that from me."

IT'S GOING TO BE TEMPTING. YOU THINK THAT just by getting it out in the open you will feel the weight of the entire world finally lift off your shoulders. I mean, why else would you have become privy to such titillating gossip if not for the chance to share it with your friends? Don't. Really. You'll be sorry if you do. Trust us. To gossip is to commit character assassination. To the character of your career, that is.

You're going to hear a lot of rumors during your tenure as an assistant. Many, many rumors. Most of which will be true. Where there's smoke there's fire, after all, and chances are that there are thousands of assistants fanning the flames on their tracking boards. This town is full of psychopaths, and psychopaths make for really good gossip material. Some of our favorite tales? Well, there's the one about the assistant who got fired for sleeping with his boss's wife. Or the one about the agent who maintains her skeletal figure by sticking to a diet of gin and opiates. And then there's the claim—it goes without saying, of course—that every male in Hollywood is really gay. Are these rumors all true? Maybe. Should you care? No.

You see, unless you're Ted Casablanca or Perez Hilton (meaning gossip is your job), a loose tongue in Hollywood amounts to a shady reputation. Once people get wind of your big mouth, they're going to be that much less likely to trust you. And why should they? You've proven

yourself to be a loose-lipped Lilly, more interested in the goings-on of people after work than the actual work. You'll seem catty, and not in the fun Heather Locklear-on-*Melrose Place* type of way. You'll also become everyone's first choice for the crown of "The Person You Cannot Trust." And don't tell us you've already forgotten what we told you about secrets before: Without any you are as useful in this town as a VHS player or a suit with shoulder pads.

"Isn't trading information pivotal to

my advancement as an industryite though?"

Yes, it is. But gossip is not information, people; it's information's juvenile assistant—chitter-chatter invented for the sole reason of making yourself feel better by making others feel worse. In other words, not cool. So button up those lips and keep the tabloid fodder where it belongs—hidden deep in your bathroom magazine rack.

TRUE CONFESSIONS

"My boss got this script from her husband at William Morris. No one could know she had it, or else the writer would risk his relationship with a certain A-list producer. I was sworn to secrecy —like if anyone found out she was reading it I'd be fired. And guess what? The producer found out. Within one day of us getting the script it was on tracking boards across town. Of course everyone immediately blamed me. My boss, her husband, the writer, the writer's assistant . . . And I only had my word to defend myself. So I sat down with my boss, looked her in the eye, and swore up and down that I wasn't the mole. And she believed me. Unbelievable, right? She even went on the record with all the other people involved saying there's no way I would be that stupid. The next day we all find out that it was her husband's driver who spilled the beans to his girlfriend who worked at a competing studio. Poor guy got the boot. Whatever, though. I was just glad my boss stuck up for me." **—L.W.**

D-Girl Now Stands for *Do-Girl*

"Did you read the new Charlie Kaufman script? It's life changing."

THERE'S THIS GIRL IN HOLLYWOOD THAT everyone knows. She's on every tracking board, goes to every mixer, reads every script, and has sex with at least three people from every top-tier agency per year. She's a **D-girl,*** and chances are her name is Heather. (D stands for development, that nebulous world where scripts "develop" into far worse versions of their former selves.)

Now, of late there's a new group of people in this town: **D-assistants.** As a normal assistant, you will be competitive, maybe even willing to go up for a job that your best friend really wants (you will tell him ahead of time of course). A D-assistant, however, takes this whole competitive thing to the next level. That is, he'll spit in your face, punch your dog, and step right on your great aunt's back in order to get that promotion. Then he'll schmooze his way into a party attended by his favorite director, go up, and ask him for a job. And finally he'll drop vicious-yet-subtle comments about your taste in front of the head of the company. "Bobby, I thought you told me you loved *Pearl Harbor.*"

YOUR MISSION: FIGHT FIRE WITH FIRE

- **You read** every script out there (or at least the coverage). Sure, you'll want to tear your hair out when you realize how untalented most writers are, but there'll come the day when you're the first to discover that gem of a script that sat on your boss's desk for the past year. (See sidebar on how to speed read, kids.)

- **You schmooze** with the bosses. Too tired to go to that **cast and crew screening** after work? Too bad. You have to put yourself in the right place to get face time with the people who can help you most.

- **You sleep** with the agents. Well, maybe skip this one. But it won't hurt your career if your S.O. happens to be the guy brokering the sale of this year's must-see film at Cannes.

Point is, don't sit back and let your peers run circles around you. Step out of your comfort zone in order to break out from the pack.

---

*Nowadays there's just as many D-boys as there are D-girls; please refrain from sending our publisher a complaint about our misogynist tendencies.

THE SECRET OF A D-GIRL'S SUCCESS: SPEED-READING, 20-10-10 STYLE

You've probably noticed them around town. You know, that girl trudging down the street, struggling up the steps of her apartment building, or trying to unlock her car door all while carrying 40 screenplays in her bag. Your first thought: "Please don't let me become one of them." Your second thought: "How in the hell is she going to read all of those scripts in one weekend?" Easy peasy, people. It's a little trick called **the 20-10-10 rule.**

As you probably know, the average screenplay runs about 120 pages long. That does not mean, however, that anyone reads all 120 pages. No, that's only if the movie is actually green-lit. For the rest of the screenplays out there, and the ones you'll probably be asked to read on a daily basis, there's no reason to read all 120 pages. Especially when you're just looking for a reason to pass. Hence, abide by the following rule:

Read the first 20 pages, then sample 10 in the middle, and finish up by reading the last 10.

With this tried and true method you will spend 20 minutes (at the most) on this piece of drivel that calls itself a script. And you'll still know everything you need to know to write the coverage or pitch the idea to Boss-man. For example:

Boss: "So what was that 'talking plant' movie about?"

You: "Ugh, it's so not even worth talking about, but it's called *Rose Red*. The gist is that the main character, an angsty loner girl in high school, finds this rose taped to her locker. She takes it home and the rose, which she nicknames Red, starts talking to her, teaching her how to exact revenge on all the jocks and cheerleaders who make fun of her every day. Loner girl becomes way popular, all thanks to the rose, which we find out at the end was placed on her locker by the loner in her math class. They all live together happily ever after."

Boss: "So it's *Little Shop of Horrors* meets *Carrie*."

You: "Exactly. But the worst possible version of each."

Boss: "Pass."

Appear Clothes Rich Even if You're Cash Poor

"Omigod, what a cute skirt! Did you get that at Neimans? I swear I just saw it on the rack somewhere . . ."

STOP! REALLY, JUST STOP. WHATEVER YOU DO, please, do not admit that you bought your outfit at Target. "Oh, who cares?" you argue. "Everyone knows I make minimum wage. They can't expect me to shop on Rodeo or something." Oh, honey, yes they can. Sure, you didn't take a job at *Vogue,* but as far as the snobs in your new office are concerned, these hallways might as well be Paris runways.

We know you're poor. So much so that you can't even afford the rent for your fleabag studio in Van Nuys without your parents' help. Add to that the fact that your financial aid payments just kicked in, your actor-wannabe boyfriend can't keep a job for more than a day, and you just adopted a child in Uzbekistan after watching a tearful Sally Struthers infomercial on TV and you, my friend, are capital B-R-O-K-E. "So please, just lighten up about the skirt. Besides, Target is busting out really fashion-forward styles lately."

Bear with us. We're not saying you can't dress for cheap. You just can't let everyone else know it. Image controls everything, and first impressions last a lifetime. That means no outfits that someone will recognize from their toiletry-shopping spree at the local Rite Aid. If you want to dress-for-less then stick to the basics: simple patterns, mix-and-match outfits, black black black. Chances are you can wear the same black pants two days in a row and no one will bat an eyelash. Sleek and simple, that's all we're saying.

"I'm not a librarian, though. I read *W* and emulate Audrey Hepburn. I was even voted best dressed all four years of high school."

Fine, because you're in luck. L.A. is full of some of the best vintage thrift stores in the country. Hit the chic-cheap joints on Melrose, check out Jet Rag on La Brea, or dive into your local Salvation Army sales bin. If the mothball smell makes you nauseated, invest in a jug of Tide.

Guys, we know you've probably fallen asleep by now, but this goes for you too. Suits are not cheap, but if you're smart you can get away with a few from the Barneys sample sale.* And cheap dress shirts can be found at department stores like Ross or Marshalls. Really, no one is going to notice that you're not wearing fine Italian silk as long as you wear it with gusto.

AVOID THE FOLLOWING WARDROBE MALFUNCTIONS . . .

T-shirts: Do not buy cotton tees for $190. This is not a good allocation of your meager funds. Spend the money on the staples (hot jeans, nice shoes) and skimp on the other stuff.

Winter: "Winter" in L.A. doesn't require all the paraphernalia you needed at that prep school in Switzerland. One nice scarf and two hip jackets and you are done. Don't buy out that cashmere rack at Fred Segal.

Jewelry: Vintage is always in. Bling it up with your grandma's antiques and the goodies you bought at the flea markets.

Hair: Never go to Supercuts. It is by no means super. That is, unless you are getting a blowout. They will blowout your hair for cheap and you can pretend you're J. Aniston for a day.

Boutiques: Go the cheapo store route instead. Target, Old Navy, The Dress Barn sales bin . . . we admit it, we've shopped at them all. So do your checking account a favor and get your basics here.

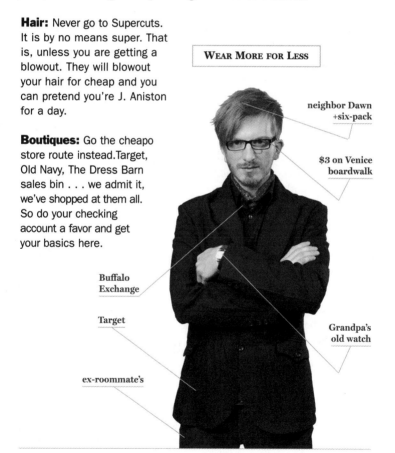

WEAR MORE FOR LESS

neighbor Dawn +six-pack

$3 on Venice boardwalk

Buffalo Exchange

Target

Grandpa's old watch

ex-roommate's

Happens in the Barker Hanger at the Santa Monica Airport at least twice annually. Bookmark this blog to keep track of not only the Barneys sale but other sample sales throughout the year: www.thebudgetfashionista.com/dish.

Get Off the Couch

"Has anyone ever tried Yogilates? Pilates alone just isn't getting at my glutes."

WE KNOW. WHEN YOU TOLD YOUR MOM YOU were moving to L.A. you promised her that you absolutely would not get sucked into the unhealthy body-conscious culture that runs this salad-obsessed city.

Too bad. You need a hot body to go along with that hot outfit of yours. Fat is not fun, and you're going to need to be in tip-top physical shape to climb the mountain of stress. That said, what better way to spend your free time than at the gym. "Ew!" you cry. "I hate you!" That's okay, we can take it. You'll love us later, especially when that company pool party rolls around and you're not getting jiggly with it.

Look, even if you don't believe that crap about a healthy mind and healthy body, there are other benefits to joining a gym. Let us enumerate a few key ones:

- **Making contacts.** Everyone you need to meet in L.A. will be at the gym. The big three: Equinox, Crunch, and Sports Club L.A. Can't afford any of these? Invoke the free two-week trial pass. With the plethora of gyms in L.A. you won't have to pay for a real membership for several months.

- **Self-esteem.** There's no better way to inspire self-confidence than having a secret weapon like a good body. When you're feeling down in the dumps, trust us, a tight behind will help pick you right back up. Suddenly feeling a little intimidated by the person interviewing you? Focusing on your six-pack for a moment will cut him down to size.

- **Watercooler workouts.** You'll be surprised how talking about workouts and body sculpting has become part of everyday conversation, on par with discussing the weather. Maybe in other cities, they discuss the economy or the latest bestseller. Here, it's abs and ass. You don't want to be the kid at the water cooler who can't tick off his top three spinning teachers.

- **Mood stabilization.** Endorphins rock, and you're gonna need 'em. Nothing pulls you out of the mild doldrums caused by long days and nights like a good four-mile beach run. Intervals with a good mix the ex threw on your iPod . . . that's the cure. And, even better, you won't need to resort to the prescription medications that all your friends have been taking. Xanax out, elliptical in.

WHERE TO BURN THE CARBS:

Yoga studios: It's no coincidence that every person leaving that level 3 Vinyasa Flow yoga class has a body you can only dream about. Step it up and get tight.

- **YogaWorks** (www.yogaworks.com): Located everywhere. They're the McDonald's of Yoga Studios. Beats a Quarter Pounder with Cheese any day.

- **Power Yoga Santa Monica** (www.poweryoga.com): Best thing about this: It's donation only. Worst thing about this: It's donation only and thus can get very, very crowded. Still, it's a workout that burns fat and soothes the soul.

- **City Yoga West Hollywood** (1067 Fairfax Ave.; www.cityyoga.com): Centrally located and you can ogle all the hot actors and actresses during child's pose.

- **YAS** (1101 Abbot Kinney Blvd., Venice; 877-YAS-YOGA; www.go2yas.com): Yoga and spinning in Venice.

Barry's Boot Camp (www.barrysbootcamp.com): The ultimate in calorie burning, almost everyone in Hollywood has tried it at one point or another. Try the Sherman Oaks or West Hollywood location. If you have to go into cardiac arrest while exercising, at least you'll get to do it while watching other hot bodies.

Chain gyms: 24-Hour Fitness, Ballys, Golds . . . You know them. Just go for the one that fits your budget.

Free: Jogging on the beach or hiking in Runyon Canyon or swimming at the Culver City Pool . . . See, being poor is no excuse for feeling like crap.

Don't Be a Snob

"I know I never called you back, but I need this favor . . . Hello??"

SOMEONE ONCE SAID THAT "HOLLYWOOD IS like high school, just with more money." This is true, but what's even more true is that the short, pimply guy who sat behind you in advanced calculus is now probably a short, less pimply (thank you, Proactiv) junior agent at ICM. Of course you didn't know that when he called you to hang out six months ago. "I can't believe he's in Hollywood," you said to yourself. "Moreover, I can't believe he's calling me. I wouldn't speak to him in sophomore year, what the hell makes him think I will talk to him now?"

So you ignored him. But now you hear he's discovered some maverick director who just won the Audience Award at Sundance. The same maverick director that your VP boss would love to attach to the rom-com your studio is trying to fast track. The same maverick director who speaks to no one but Mr. Pimpleface from high school. Crap. Crap. Crap. That's right, let's see if he returns your call now.

In the real world, you can write people off. That college friend who came to town and never called you? Gone. The boyfriend who said those pair of jeans made you look "hippy"? See ya. The colleague you despise but has excellent taste and an A-list reputation? "Hello! How are you?? Oh my god, it's so good to see you again!"

Yes, you'll vomit as these words come out of your mouth. Yes, you'll question your character and moral fiber. And yes, you'll ask your friends from home if you have become one of those "awful Hollywood types" you promised yourself you'd never be. (They'll respond in the affirmative.) Rest assured, though. This isn't the real you talking. This is the Biz talking.

★ *Nerd's the word.*

Remember how you didn't tell Krissy the head cheerleader to go to hell for fear of getting blacklisted from the prom? Same thing here. You simply must call back the dweeb who wants to talk directors over mai tais. Still not convinced? Then think of the time spent on this random drink (one hour, people!) as a game of poker. Just one good hand and it could pay dividends that you never thought possible. You don't have to invite him to your Thursday drinking group, but make him feel special and important for an hour. Hell, at least you'll be able to numb the pain with rum.

WHAM, BAM, THANK YOU, STAN: HOW TO MAKE PAINFUL DRINK REQUESTS LESS PAINFUL

The Case of the Lonely Coworker:
The girl who went to your college now works down the hall and thinks it would be a hoot to spend Saturdays shopping together on Larchmont *after* going to brunch and getting buy-one-get-one-free manicures. Okay, this is a case of something we like to call overkill drinks. Networking via drinks is not an all-day event. After all, you barely see your friends so you're not going to spend all weekend bonding with someone you don't like.

Solution: Tell her that your weekends are packed (first aid training, tae kwon do certification, mentoring an at-risk student, etc.). "I'd love to do a lunch during the workweek though."

The Case of the Eager Interns:
Each one of your 12 interns wants to take you out for dinner. You feel like you need to say yes. After all, they are working for you for free. The least you can do is spend an hour giving them career advice.

Solution: Organize one big dinner. Ask the boss if you can expense it (you'll go somewhere cheap, à la Barney's Beanery*), pick a date for the end of the semester, and get it all done with in one big bang.

The Case of the Distant Relative:
Relatives come out of the woodwork when you get a job in Hollywood. All of a sudden your favorite professor's son, boss's niece, and vet's cousin will be asking you for a "sit-down." They're smart to do so, after all. We told you to do the same thing when you were first starting out. However, chances are that unless you want a second career as a headhunter, you'll want to run the other way.

Solution: The Phone Call. Have the wannabes call you during work hours and quickly tell them everything they need to know over the phone. Before they know it you'll be saying good-bye and wishing them the best of luck with their job search, and you have done your good deed.

The Case of the Becky Brigade:
That chick from your tracking group sends the following e-mail: "We're all going salsa dancing and then Becky got us on the list at the new Brent Bolthouse club! You're coming, right?" We know. You just want to crawl up in your room and watch *Dawson's Creek,* seasons 1 and 2, not hang out with Becky and her D-girl disaster friends.

Solution: Go for one drink. That's all. Because if you miss out on too many of these puppies, the Becky Brigade will not only stop inviting you, they'll start bad-mouthing you. And with their stellar networking skills, all of Hollywood will soon know you spend your Saturday nights watching Dawson pine over Joey.

---

*8447 Santa Monica Blvd.; 323-654-2287; www.barneysbeanery.com

Stick with the Pack

"Did you hear Joanne is angling for the Lionsgate job I told her about? She is so dead meat."

NOW MAYBE THAT LAST RULE ISN'T SITTING right with you. "I didn't come to Hollywood to make friends. I came to win!" Okay, we get that, which is why we're going to reiterate it in this rule. But first, look around you. There are dozens of other assistants sitting next to you who are thinking exactly the same thing. Every day you size each of them up, weighing your strengths and weaknesses against theirs. "Does she know more people than me?" "Do people think he has better taste?" "Why does my boss always say hello to that snot across the hall when he won't even look in my direction??"

Are you a bad person for being competitive? Don't be ridiculous. You have no choice, in any case. Only a handful of you will make it to the next level, whether that's as a junior agent, creative executive, casting associate, etc. The rest will be relegated to the B list of Hollywood jobs. Think home video department, below-the-line agency, and starter-wifehood. Let's not even talk about the thousands who flee Hollywood to go manage the Applebee's in North Carolina. Yes, this is based on a true story.

Now, some of you might think that the only way to outshine the competition is to draw attention to yourself. Whether this is positive or negative attention doesn't matter. You just want the boss to recognize your quick wit and stellar taste. As for what the other assistants think? "Let them eat cake."

Well, let's set the record straight: A superiority complex does not a future executive make. Pissing off your fellow assistants is just plain stupid. You might as well pin a target to your back that says "Going Nowhere," because you're a goner as long as you carry an attitude like that.

Think you're special because you just graduated from the Stark program? Try telling that to the Harvard Law School grad who's spent the last ten months pushing a mail cart at Paradigm. Feel like you deserve preferential treatment because your father ran Columbia many moons ago? Well, I'm sure the copy machine will be really interested in that story when tray 3 jams on you for the eighth time today. The truth is, no matter where you went to school or how cinematically minded you think you are, you will need your fellow assistants to push you to the top of the Hollywood Heap. By separating yourself, you are simply welcoming their scorn. What will result is a feeding frenzy for your demise. The people you once thought powerless and beneath you will eat you for dinner. Rumors about your small you-know-what will spread like wildfire across the tracking boards. Coworkers will tell their bosses stories about your, UH OH, bad taste. "Oh god, please stop! Please, I beg of you, I can't take it anymore!!!" Okay, just chill. We've got your back as long as you've got ours. But stop the showboating already.

TRUE CONFESSIONS

"I had to hire him. He was my boss's fourth cousin twice removed and he wanted an internship during his summer break from Harvard. In my mind that meant making him do what I did when I was an intern—copy scripts, file headshots, and fetch green tea blendeds from Starbucks. But then he showed up that first day, asking where his office was, and I knew I was in deep s#%$. This kid, now forever known as IFH (Intern from Hell), was evil. He literally said things like, 'I'd never be an assistant. It's such a bitch move." Or "Do you enjoy being a secretary?" The dude thought he was above being an assistant, and by repeatedly saying this out loud, he pissed off the entire office. I cracked open a bottle of Dom that was in my boss's closet when IFH finally had to go back to school. Cut to the next summer. I get a call from some H.R. person at Fox asking me what I thought of IFH who, how ironic, was applying to be an *assistant*. Now don't get me wrong, I never said, 'Don't hire him, he sucks,' but I did drop subtle hints about his less than stellar work ethic. 'Do I think he's a hard worker? He's average. Do I think he'd fit in at a studio? Actually I don't think I'm qualified to answer that . . .' Things like that. Sorry if that sounds harsh, but this kid did it to himself." **—G.A.**

Think Drink

"I love the nightlife."

EVERY KID IN THIS TOWN LOVES THE nightlife. It's no wonder you do as well. Just look at the lines outside the sunset Strip on a Monday night and you might wonder if anyone in Hollywood has an actual job they have to wake up for tomorrow morning. Damn those trust fund babies.

Alas, part of your new life in Hollywood is going out. Assistant mixers, one-on-one drinks, meet-and-greets . . . By the time Friday night rolls around you won't want to see the top of a bar stool ever again. Some assistants love this. After all, about 50 percent of the people who claim they want to make movies for a living really just want to be around movies, and by movies they mean the parties, the obscenely good-looking celebs, and the $100 bills falling from the sky.

"But I hate making small talk!" Too bad. In a business where *who* you know is more important than *what* you know, you will have to master it. You'll need to meet other assistants if you want to be able to gather that all-important tidbit that will impress your boss. That script from last year's Best Screenplay winner that no other producer in town can get his hands on? Guess what? You went out for drinks with her boyfriend and he's more than happy to e-mail it to you. Getting your boss into the hottest new lounge bar? Also no problem. You picked up the tab on her two vodka tonics a month ago.

Also, let's not forget that some of the most notorious deals in Hollywood have been brokered over a few rounds of drinks. Harvey and Bob Weinstein agreed to buy *sex, lies, and videotape* for $1 million while boozing it up at Sundance (the movie grossed $25 million, thereby launching the idea that independent film could be profitable, thereby causing the downfall of independent film. But we digress). Spielberg, Katzenberg, and Geffen dreamt up the whole DreamWorks SKG thing over several dinners at Morton's. Tom Cruise interviewed all his potential wives over martinis at the Hotel Bel-Air. (Okay, we made that one up.) Point is, there is no distinction between socializing and negotiating. No wonder this town has more than its fair share of drinking problems.

WARNING! Don't be the promiscuous networker. This is the dude who asks every assistant in town out for drinks. This doesn't mean you can avoid asking others out for a drink though. You must. And you must pretend to love it. It's called net*working* after all, not net*havingsomuchfun*.

THE FINE ART OF "DRINKS"

Doing drinks in Hollywood is an age-old custom, as time tested as studio publicity departments covering up their teen starlets' pill-popping habits. Point is, you will find yourself "on drinks" at least once a week, if not every day. Is there proper etiquette to such an event? We're so glad you asked.

BEST BARS FOR DRINKS:

1. Hotel Bars

Why? They exude class. But here's your fair warning: **That cocktail is gonna run you $15.**

Faves: Four Seasons, L'Ermitage, Maison 140, The Avalon

Definitely No: Skybar at The Mondrian (way too cliché)

2. Pseudo Dive Bars

Why? Casual and comfortable, yet the clientele doesn't smell.

Faves: El Carmen, St. Nicks, The Other Room, The Arsenal

Definitely No: The Saddle Ranch (screams Valley)

3. Chains That We Condone (if you must)

Why? **Sometimes you just need comfort food.**

Faves: Houstons, Trader Vic's, McCormick & Schmick's

Definitely No: Islands (it's L.A., not the Bahamas)

Drink Recommendations:

The only rule: Drink above your means.

What this means: Champagne, single-malt Scotch, high-end vodka, sake (cold, not warm).

Drinks That You Will Be Tempted by But Should Never Order:
Apple martini: Very 1999.

Anything that needs to be blended: Have you tried having a conversation over a blender?

Anything that comes in a takeaway mug: You don't want to project "Las Vegas tourist."

Anything that glows, flames, or has a risqué name, like Fuzzy Nipple: Very Phi Sig toga party.

Well liquor: There's no need to let the world know you're poor.

Tap water: If you're on the wagon at least go for something bubbly (i.e., San Pellegrino) so as not to seem cheap.

Maximum Number of Drinks to Have on Drinks:

Two! That's all. There's nothing worse than the drinks date who gets sloshed and spends the whole night confessing her sexual obsession with her boss or what he learned about Mum in last week's therapy session.

P.S. Don't suggest a bar way on the opposite side of town just because that's where you live (i.e., Big Foot Lodge in Atwater). That would be rude.

"You can e-mail everyone in my company by typing 'all staff' as the e-mail address. Usually people use this feature for lame things like, 'Please watch the wet paint in the third floor stairwell' or 'Come to Kayla's birthday party at 4 P.M.' Once, though, one of the senior executives intending to send a message to her friend Ally accidentally sent the very private e-mail to 'all staff.' It was about her blind date the night before, and let's just say it was NSFW.* The date included binge-drinking, strippers, and a dirty act inside a bathroom stall that I'd rather not repeat. Ten minutes after the e-mail reached all our in-boxes, the exec's assistant sent the following e-mail: 'Please know that the previous e-mail from my boss, subject entitled "Up all night," was actually from me. I accidentally typed it from my boss's mailbox. All contents relate to *my* blind date last night, *not* my boss's. I apologize for the inappropriate and unprofessional content. I will be more discreet in the future.' In typical Hollywood fashion, the assistant actually benefited from the bad rep. The guys in the office all wanted her and the girls all wanted to be around her, at least to leach off her leftovers." **—B.V.**

*Not safe for work

TRUE CONFESSIONS

Flirt with Class

"Have you ever talked to Kevin at MGM? He gives such good phone."

PERHAPS THE GREATEST SIMPLE PLEASURE resulting from Hollywood's over-reliance on phones is flirting. On any given day you will talk to approximately 60 other assistants, which also translates into 60 opportunities to flirt. "Um, but dude, I only flirt with girls." Yeah, right, we've heard that one before. Our point is this: If you want to make it in this town, you better start flirting with everyone you speak to over the phone. Guys, girls, old ladies, old agents . . . it doesn't matter. Just flirt.

- The first thing you'll need to master is your voice. Some of you were blessed with a naturally sexy voice, on a par with Lauren Bacall or Denzel Washington. Most of you, however, will need some help. First thing you need to do is listen to yourself. Practice by recording your voicemail message over and over. If all else fails, resort to the whisper. Everyone sounds good a little breathy.

- Next up, your tone. Sure you're stressed out and pissed off, but never let the person on the other end of the line know this. You must answer every call like you've just walked into the mansion after a lovely day at Carbon Beach (in the 'Bu, of course). You are calm, relaxed, and beyond joyful to be stranded at your desk picking the pennies out of your boss's change jar (lunch money). Your fellow phone flirts will be impressed by your natural ease. Way to go, doll.

- Third, be open to chitchat. No sane person can work for 12 hours straight. You must take a break for yourself every once in awhile so why not take a moment to get to know the voice on the other end of your phone. Hate small talk? Fine, then. Try to work them for some gossip. Hate gossip? Better go get that degree in Astrophysics. You're in the wrong business.

WARNING! Beware the face-to-face meeting. Take it from us. Personal experience has proven that the one with the best phone voice often ends up with the worst outward appearance. Maybe it's God's way of balancing the scales of fate but, whatever you do, do not expect a sexy voice to correlate with a sexy body. Otherwise you'll be way disappointed when you show up at Tom Bergin's* for a drink.

An old Irish pub in a city that tries to kill all things old, Tom Bergin's (840 S. Fairfax; 323-936-7151; www.tombergins.com) is a staple of the beer scene. Bonus: Kiefer Sutherland is a regular.

Don't Overmix

"Assistant mixers are fun, ya'll!"

LISTEN UP ALL YOU OVER-EAGER ASSISTANTS out there. Organizing an event where tired assistants are forced to hang out with other tired assistants in a contrived-yet-somewhat-fascinating-because-it-is-so-pathetic setting is not cool. "But I want to meet that girl Ronna at Sony who sounds so hot over the phone." Oh, stop whining. If you must attend one of these mixers, even if it's just to see firsthand how god-awful an experience it can be, please follow our advice below. Oh, and just a warning, Ronna is *not* going to be hot. I thought we already told you that—the sexy-sounding ones never are.

HOW TO NOT COMMIT SUICIDE WHEN YOU FIND YOURSELF AT AN ASSISTANT MIXER:

1. **Find the bar.** That's right, don't stop to get your nametag, collect your gift bag, or talk to that girl at ICM you met a few months back. Just make a beeline for the bar because you're going to need at least two shots to make it through the next half hour. Just pray that the schmuck who organized this thing was savvy enough to have Grey Goose sponsor your drinking habit.

2. **Avoid the buffet.** Sure, you haven't eaten since sneaking some of your boss's french fries at lunch and those shots at the bar seem to be making you a tad loopy. Whatever you do, do not eat the free food. One, you will get sick. Two, the bathrooms at these mixers are never sit-down-friendly. Three, everyone will see you as weak. After all, only sad people eat carbs after seven.

3. Bring an entourage. There's nothing weirder than the assistant who shows up to a mixer alone. I mean, did you actually expect to meet people at this thing? As if! Better that you bring a friend, find a nice corner, and make fun of all the other people there. Besides, no one is going to want to talk to the freak that doesn't know anyone, even if you are Jerry Bruckheimer's first assistant.

4. Arrive late, leave early. Okay, maybe there is something weirder than going to a mixer alone, and that would be staying there for the duration. You want to do one hour max at a mixer, at least so it looks like you have better things to do (pop over to Colin Farrell's pad for a nightcap, for example). The exception? If you fall in love. Really, there's no other excuse for closing out the mixer.

5. Be nice, but not too nice. We hate the snob who is way too cool for school to look us in the eye when we meet her. What we hate more: the overfriendly geek so desperate to be our friend that we have a feeling he'd let us write derogatory statements on his forehead with a Sharpie if we just asked nicely. Instead, master the art of polite detachment. You will seem all the more confident, not to mention mysterious, for it.

Get an Entourage

"Who needs Tony Soprano when I've got my best bud Pauly that works at UTA?"

WHETHER YOU'RE ITALIAN, ASIAN, GAY, RED-headed, a pothead, or just have some friends with a common sense of humor, you need to create your very own posse. Look at all the people who've reached great heights in Tinseltown. The Coppola family. The über-agents who created CAA. The Arquettes. Okay, maybe that's pushing it. Our point is that most of these people would never have stepped foot on a studio lot if it wasn't for the vast network of friends and family pushing them through the system.

The same goes for you. Alone, you are an industry pariah whom people will ignore and talk smack about. Surrounded by comrades, however, you are irresistible. Popular beyond belief. Remember: high school with money. So even if people don't like you, they'll think they should when you roll into Dan Tana's* with your crew of homies.

The simple truth is that no one can succeed in this industry—or any business—alone. In Hollywood, you need strength in numbers if you're going to survive, let alone make it past the velvet rope at Geisha House. That means friends who can tell you about better jobs, who can back you up when you bitch-slap that dude at The Grove, and who tell you when your butt is getting too big to fit in your BMW coupe.

ALL IN THE FAMILIES

Here are some of Hollywood's most significant clans:

Family Mafias: We mentioned a few before, but there's also the Huvane Brothers (Kevin heads CAA, Stephen's a partner at PMK, and Chris is an editor at *GQ*); the Redgrave Ladies (Vanessa, Lynn, Joely Richardson, Natasha Richardson. Can we please get someone to bottle this acting gene?); the Wayans Family (Keenan, Damon, Shawn, Marlon, Kim . . . they win hands down).

Colleges: USC, Brown, Stanford, Wisconsin, Penn . . . The list goes

---

*Founded in 1964, Dan Tana's (310-275-9444; www.dantanasrestaurant.com) has become one of Hollywood's most venerable haunts. Just ask Drew Barrymore, who says she had her diapers changed here. Both cozy and celeb-heavy, you're just as likely to swoon over the fab chicken parmigiana as overhear Larry King's conversation with Rupert Murdoch in the corner booth. The catch? Scoring a res is hard. Dan Tana's core customers, after all, are their own mafia.

on and on. So what if you couldn't stand all your classmates back then? Now you're president of the Alumni Entertainment Group.

Sports: Ice hockey, softball, cycling, surfing. HPPs play as hard as they work.

★ *Cliques are not just for high school.*

Gay Mafia: Although Michael Ovitz was reamed for outing this gang in a 2002 *Vanity Fair* interview, he wasn't lying. It exists. (Lloyd from *Entourage,* bless his heart, is even a member of the junior version, "The Gay Assistants Corps.") Sorry, no heteros allowed in this club.

Friends of Bill (aka Alcoholics Anonymous): Hollywood peeps are notorious for their hard-partying ways. Subsequently, many end up in this mafia which, to be honest, is probably not one its members want you shouting about in the streets.

Poker: There's no easier way to befriend Tobey Maguire than by ending up to the right of him at your friend's weekly poker game. At this table, everyone is equal.

Scientology: Tom and Katie, the Travoltas, Kirstie Alley, Jenna Elfman, Beck, Paul Haggis . . . 'Nuff said.

Supersize Your Confidence

"Ugh, I'm so exhausted. I've got like three movies shooting right now."

UM, NO YOU DON'T. YOUR *BOSS* HAS THREE movies shooting right now. And no, the short you made with your DV cam last Sunday doesn't count.

One of our biggest pet peeves in the Biz is people stretching the truth. Not self-promoting, not patting themselves on the back, but serving straight up McTruths. And people do it all the time. Some execs, for instance, exaggerate everything from their personal worth to their client's last paycheck to their job title (our favorite: Junior Director of Story Editing. Please—we don't even know what that means).

Assistants are no different. Even the lowliest will serve you an Egg McTruth with a side of Lies on a daily basis. The Wiz at the management company will tell you he's best friends with Jake Gyllenhaal, the eager beaver on the set will say he's running all of Second Unit, and Princess at the studio will brag that she basically runs the lot.

Every assistant exaggerates a little, but there comes a point where your exaggeration becomes delusional. Sure, we believe that you talk to Jake G. on the phone (i.e., "Please hold"), but we're not buying that you surf together on the weekends. Maybe you went surfing at the same time as him, but the fact that he was 15 miles up the coast at Zuma Beach does not count as actual "hang time." This behavior makes it seem like you're uncomfortable with your second-class Hollywood citizenship. How do you think it makes all of your fellow assistants feel that you are embarrassed to be an assistant? Hmm, let's see . . . Pathetic, hurt, annoyed, belittled, resentful, and finally: REALLY sick of you.

But what's even worse is when you pretend like you *are* your boss. Because guess what? You're not. Please stop calling your friends and saying things like, "Wow, we just negotiated this killer backend for the Pittster." Right, because Brad Pitt even knows you exist. Last time he was in the office he called you Chuck. Your name is Phyllis.

Our solution: Cut the crap. We know there are those times in the job where you may exhibit brilliant thinking, but it ain't your name on the screen yet, DeMille. You are a schlepper. Really. It won't be this way forever, but as of now, this very moment, you are not an executive. You're just trying to be one.

WARNING: DO NOT ATTEMPT TO USE
ANY OF THE FOLLOWING McTRUTHS

THE HANDBAG McTRUTH: "Doll, you must check out my new Gucci bag. To die for, right? Of course I can't afford it but I said to myself, 'Girl, treat yourself, you deserve it.'"

The dirty truth: Girl, you bought the bag from Josefina on Sixth Street. Who, by the way, does a stellar job considering she's raising three kids and working two other jobs between stitching these puppies.

The solution: If you're called out on your knockoff, fess up. There's no shame in not spending $3K on something that exists solely to hold old receipts and lipsticks. A-plus for effort, though.

THE BUSY McTRUTH: "So sorry I never called you back. I don't even have time to eat! Work has been soooo busy lately."

The dirty truth: Soooo busy, huh? How about that hour you spent reading *In Touch* this morning? We have news for you, Busy Phillips. Telling someone you're too busy to call him back is a slap in the face. You're basically saying that, out of all the things on your to-do list, he falls on the very bottom rung. Right there with writing that thank-you note to Grammy Pearl for the sweater adorned with labradoodles she knitted you last Christmas.

The solution: Please, can we retire the "I'm busy" line already? Let's just start telling our friends the truth: "I've been a jerk," "I got preoccupied with work," or even "I'm over you."

THE TRAVEL McTRUTH: "I can't believe how much traveling I have to do this month. I'm already exhausted."

The dirty truth: You and all that "traveling"? Right, because we heard one trip was to the Valley to pick up special shampoo for your balding boss, another was to Bakersfield for your grandpa's 70th, and the last was across the street to Jamba Juice for your boss's daily wheatgrass shot.

The solution: As long as you're working as an assistant, everyone knows your jet-setting lifestyle is permanently grounded. There's no need to act like something you're not.

THE FOOD McTRUTH: "I haven't eaten a carb in like 13 days."

The dirty truth: What about that slice of Sweet Lady Jane German chocolate cake we saw you wolf down at Chad's birthday party? And the mini cupcakes at staff lunch? Sure they were small, but those had crème fraiche in them, pumpkin. Or the seven margaritas at El Cholo last night? Hate to tell ya this, but those were all McCarbs.

The solution: Stop talking about food. Sure, you can think about it, but do what A-list actresses do and keep your food issues to your neurotic self.

Think Before You Speak

"What do I truly think, boss? I think your brother's script stinks."

YOU'VE BEEN WORKING THE DESK FOR SIX OR seven months now, you've got the phone sheet mastered, and your boss thinks you're a total star. However, you still haven't met the owner of the company (he spends most of his time off the coast of Greece) and you're a bit nervous about your first all-staff lunch. It's your big chance to distinguish yourself from all the other faceless assistants. So you show up, pen and paper primed to take notes, and not two minutes later the CEO's looking right at you:

"Who here has anything to say about the *Commando Princess* project?"

Silence. Just the sound of crickets. You can't believe it. No one is speaking up. Not even your senior VP boss. That is weak, if not just rude. So you open your mouth: "Well, I think the script needs work. Not only do we not understand why she's fleeing the Lebanese rebels, but there's no real character development. Why does she tell her father that he's dead to her? Why does she feel the need to sleep with every peasant boy she encounters? And let's be honest, the third act is a complete mess. We completely lose our arc."

You take a breath, proud of yourself for being so articulate. But then you see it. On Big Boss Man's forehead. A vein pulsating like an angry worm. "You. OUT!!!" Yup, you've come down with a little case of foot-in-mouth disease. Here's how to prevent another outbreak:

Rule 1: Avoid public displays of opinion. Never use a staff meeting to make your first big splash. Even if you're brilliant, it'll come across as obnoxious.

Rule 2: Start at the bottom. Begin by sharing your thoughts with your peers, whether that's the interns, other assistants, or your low-level boss. You'll get a taste test of how they respond to your opinions.

Rule 3: Know thy audience. Take into account to whom you're about to offer your opinion. You might love a script to death, but you can't say that if the writer happens to be the dude who slept with your boss's wife, even if that encounter predated the boss's marriage.

Rule 4: Beware the too-strong opinion. You don't want to look like a Fool when that script you belittled becomes next year's *My Big Fat Greek Wedding*.

A TRUE STORY FROM THE TRENCHES: THE CASE OF THE OBNOXIOUS MOVIE-QUOTER GUY

This lesson reminds us of a certain type of guy. You know him. He knows every line in every movie since the inception of the talkies, and he's ready to recite them to every studio chief he meets. News flash, Mikey: If you land a job at a reasonably competent company with a somewhat intelligent boss, chances are she too has seen a lot of movies. So don't be the guy on coffee break who thinks it's cool to quote *Top Gun*—"Can you grab me a creamer?" "That's a negative, Ghostrider, the pattern is full"—instead of actually forming your own sentences. For instance:

Coworker: Mikey, will you please clean up your dirty
dishes in the kitchen?
Mikey: You talkin' to me?
Coworker: (big sigh): Yes, Mikey, I'm talking to you.
Mikey: You talkin' to ME?!

STOP! Enough already. Or we're officially done with you.

★ *De Niro gets to say it, not you.*

Avoid Boss Traps

"She asked you to do what? And you did WHAT?? Oh. My. God."

PSST. YES, YOU—OVER HERE. COME CLOSER. Did you hear about that girl? You know, the one who went over to her boss's house on a Saturday night, only to end up pregnant, fat, and alone? Yeah, us too. Thank god we know better.

Believe it or not, some sordid stuff happens in the City of Angels. Whether it's movie stars picking up prostitutes, not-yet-legal starlets downing alcohol in public, or stage moms making their eight-year-olds get plastic surgery, you can pretty much expect to witness the worst of human behavior. It should also come as no surprise then that bosses sometimes sleep with their assistants. "That's like, *so* illegal!!" Yeah, go tell that to Rickie (a pseudonym, of course; we'd never gossip using real names), who slept his way to a partner position over at the agency.

Obviously, not all bosses sleep with their assistants. No, just the really lonely ones. Chances are you or a friend or a long lost cousin will be propositioned at one point or other. Sometimes it can be subtle, other times not so much. For example, your boss might say, "Please bring me that file on the Houdini Project." Which is totally appropriate. *Except* when the Houdini Project is actually code for a very extensive collection of photos of your naked boss. (Trust us, do *not* open this file.)

We see you're rolling your eyes at this point. You already know that people are perverts and figured out how to deal with them way back in college, thank you very much. So we're babying you. Let's just set the record straight, then. It's not that you don't know how to deal with the pervs, it's that you might not want to. That's right—you might be tempted to give in. Power mixed with money and a semiattractive boss can be intoxicating. You might find yourself thinking, "Well, maybe he's sort of cute, and he is a super-powerful producer. I guess I could get over the weight problem . . ." Don't worry, though, this isn't the real you talking; it's just a side effect of the Kool-Aid you drank when you agreed to work in this screwy town in the first place.

Here are some ways to ward off the dirty dreams and, god forbid, acting on them:

■ **Don't oversocialize with your boss.** Sure, it's okay for you to hang outside the office, but limit yourself to more platonic settings. That means no working out together, no stopping by the house past midnight, and definitely no getting tanked together in some divey Mexican restaurant. We've seen way too many assistants fall prey to a boss after a few too many margaritas at El Coyote.*

- **Dress like a professional.** Guys, this means long sleeves. Girls, ditch the miniskirt. Naked flesh is great for the big screen, not the office in Century City.
- **Practice prudence.** We know, you're laughing at this one. But the minute you give your boss the a-okay about flirting, the closer you are to becoming a goner. Put on the prim and proper puss.

POP QUIZ: WHICH ONE OF THE BELOW IS A DECENT PROPOSAL?

a. "Pick up Amber from Jumbo's Clown Room."**

b. "Compile research on the porn industry."

c. "Call my wife and tell her about the diet that worked so well for your backside."

d. "Accompany me to this Oscar party."

e. "Can you bring that ruler over here? I need you to measure something."

Answer: b. Projects about porn are in right now. Besides, a little research never hurt anyone.

Eating at El Coyote is a rite of passage for any L.A. newbie. Both centrally located and el cheapo, the menu is filled with all that greasy cheesy goodness you need to nurse a hangover. Beware though, those seemingly smooth house margaritas are proven hallucinogens (7312 Beverly Blvd.; 523-939-2255).

**Jumbo's (5153 Hollywood Blvd.; 323-666-1187; www.jumbos.com) is indeed a strip joint. But a strip joint like no other. Very David Lynch territory. Enter at your own risk.*

Party at Your Own Risk

"Are you going to the premiere? I'm so getting trashed!"

BOOZING IT UP AT A COMPANY EVENT? CLASSY. Really classy. Sleeping with the boss isn't the only indiscretion to be guarded against. You're going to be tempted to give in to your craziest whims and desires at work functions, as well. Our advice: Don't.

Take the company holiday party. The CEO has invited everyone to his 24-bedroom mansion in Bel-Air. DJ AM is going to be spinning and the open bar is hosted by Veuve. The company COO even sent out an e-mail saying this is your time to celebrate, relax, and enjoy the fruits of your labor. "Score!" you think. "I'm totally cabbing it home with that hot number Cassie from the Accounting department. Another round of Patrón shots over here." Not so fast, big guy. You see, although they say they want you to enjoy yourself, this isn't your sister's wedding. Binge drinking, sloppy behavior, and public displays of affection must be kept to a minimum. Otherwise you'll show up for work on Monday to find a temp sitting at your desk and Lou from Security waiting to escort you from the building.

Believe us, we've seen a lot of crazy things go on at these parties—executives slugging whiskey from the bottle, 60-year-old secretaries busting a move to "Thong Song," and interns giving free lap dances to those waiting in the port-o-potty line. And we were horrified. Okay, we were enthralled. But not in a good way. Because we knew, no boss was going to promote the loose cannon who couldn't show even the slight-

est self-control at a company event. Hence, limit yourself to a two-vice minimum. That means the number of vodka and Red Bulls you can drink, girls you're allowed to hit on, and songs you can butcher on the karaoke machine. "I'd like to dedicate this next song to Cassie in Accounting." Beat. "All by myseeeelf. Don't wanna be, all by myyyy-seeeelf, ANYMOOOOOOORE . . ." Ouch, our ears still hurt just thinking about it.

POP QUIZ! WHICH ONE OF THE FOLLOWING IS APPROPRIATE COMPANY PARTY BEHAVIOR?

a. **Dancing to the Electric Slide**

b. **Karaoking to "I Touch Myself"**

c. **Gorging on free sushi**

d. **Playing beer pong**

e. **French-kissing your coworker**

f. **Photocopying body parts**

g. **Dressing in drag**

h. **Wrestling with Ashley, the boss's pit bull**

i. **Jumping into the pool with the folks from Accounts Receivable**

j. **Flirting with the CEO's spouse**

k. **Standing in the corner the entire time**

l. **Chatting only to your superiors**

m. **Chatting only to the waiters**

Answer: h. Sucking up to the boss's pet is a sure-fire way to snag the corner office. The rest of these are just tacky.

TRUE CONFESSIONS

"It was my first premiere. I was working as an assistant for a producer and had slaved away on the movie—late nights, endless weekends, assisting all the big guns on whatever they needed, you name it. I was just glad to be done with it all. So I bought a new tube top and headed to the Chinese for the premiere. So many celebs, my name in the credits, the open bar ...It was all pretty overwhelming. I think it was around my sixth apple martini when my boyfriend told me it was time to go. I was like, 'But now we go to the after party. And I still have to tell Cameron how good she was.' He was like, 'You're going nowhere but home, sweetie.' It took him half an hour to find a cab. I apparently used this time to empty my stomach by the limo stand. Showing my face at work the next morning was pretty brutal. The other assistants thought it would be funny to host a mock intervention during lunch. Even my boss was in on it. 'We're worried about you, S. Last night was clearly a cry for help. Have you seen *When a Man Loves a Woman*?' I was able to laugh about it by the end of the day but still—the shame, the shame." **—S.B.**

THE TINSELTOWN TEST: TAKE 4

16. It's your first time in front of the president of the company and he wants to know everyone's opinion on the most recent cut of the *Jaws* remake. You take this as an opportunity to . . .

a. introduce yourself.

b. blend in unnoticed.

c. tell your idea on how to fix the third act.

d. alert him to the poor working conditions of the office.

e. None of the above.

17. Some assistant keeps making sexual innuendo jokes on the phone to you. You respond by . . .

a. making sexual innuendo jokes back.

b. threatening legal action.

c. fantasizing about your first meeting.

d. keeping it professional.

18. The twerp in the mailroom keeps pushing your requests to the bottom of the pile. In order to reconcile the situation, you . . .

a. scream profanities.

b. arrange a professional sit-down.

c. act sugary sweet.

d. call Human Resources.

19. The assistant mixer you're at is actually turning out to be tons o' fun. You . . .

a. get your third drink at the bar.

b. make out with the assistant who eyed you across the appetizer table.

c. leave, saying you've got to do notes on three scripts.

d. let your friends leave without you, knowing you can get a ride home from that nerd you know from NYU.

e. None of the above.

20. You're exhausted and can't wait to go home and watch *Golden Girls* reruns when a fellow assistant invites you to karaoke night. You . . .

a. accept, but refrain from taking the stage during their "Sweet Caroline" group number.

b. accept, doing your best rendition of "Baby's Got Back."

c. pass and read a script instead.

d. pass and park it on the sofa with Blanche and Rose whilst pretending to read a script.

ANSWERS: 16. b; **17.** a; **18.** c; **19.** c; **20.** a

TAKE 5:
AWARDS SEASON

WOW, THIS IS AMAZING. TRULY. YOU'RE NEAR THE END OF THIS 26-mile marathon. You can see the finish line on the horizon, hear the crowds cheering, and taste the delectable protein bar waiting for you at the finish line . . . But the hardest miles of all are ahead. You might be tempted to give up. To stop, lie down on the side of the road, and sleep . . .

No you won't, mister. You have come this far, and for that you should be proud. Because if you stop here on your journey to be an executive, you will end up a **lifer** (aka career assistant, but more on them later)—and, as we recall, a lifetime of answering phones was not on the Wish List that we had you make at the beginning of this journey. No, you wanted to win an Academy Award (or make a few million bucks, or run a studio, or direct movies with a message . . .). Whatever your dream, it is only by continuing with our lessons that you will have a chance to achieve it. You are now ready to enter the final stage of your career as an assistant: AWARDS SEASON.

The following rules provide the precious nuggets of wisdom you'll need to parlay this assistant gig into a real promotion—tips about asking for a raise, begging your boss for more work, and knowing the one big secret to make it to the next level. These will be the hardest lessons to follow and, as such, will provide the biggest reward thus far—a career.

Cowards Go Home

"I did notes on every script, mixed at every assistant mixer, and spent three years working for the President of Production. Now where's that promotion?"

THERE USED TO BE A TIME IN HOLLYWOOD when it was much easier to move up the studio ladder. You put in your time as an assistant, read all the best scripts, canoodled with all the right people, and waited to be promoted. Done and dusted. But not any more. Moviemaking—no matter if you're working in the studio system or the indy nonsystem—is a nebulous world, so much so that sometimes you'll wonder if who succeeds and who doesn't is a matter of luck. Well, it's not. Luck helps, sure, but it doesn't smile on the faint of heart. Trust us, when that schmuck who sat next to you for six months—you know, the one who thought Paul Newman was famous only for his spaghetti sauce but always bulldozed his way into story meetings—gets promoted to story editor before you do, the lesson will be abundantly clear. Hence, now that you've got some experience, it's time for you to think outside the box.

Sure, a master's from Stark* is a good way to get your foot in the door. So is having a grandfather who used to run MGM. As well as an uncanny knack for understanding the **three-act structure.** But none of this means anything unless you've got the guts to make bold decisions.

Hollywood, as I'm sure you've figured out by now, is run by mavericks. All HPPs knew early in their careers that they'd have to forge their own paths if they were to become truly successful. Harvey Weinstein got his start promoting music concerts. Sherry Lansing was a model/actress/schoolteacher. Steven Spielberg dropped out of college (only to get his degree 20-odd years later). And what do all these people have in common? Their big, giant-sized balls. Well, balls mixed with ingenuity, hard work, and passion.

No HPP came to Hollywood simply to make a decent living; rather, they came to leave their mark on the world, and what better way to do that than work in one of the most powerful mediums out there? By the way, it is this exact passion, this courage, that we revere in our favorite

The Stark Producing Program at USC is famous for building the next generation of HPPs. Alums include writers like John Wells (ER) and John August (the most recent Charlie and the Chocolate Factory), producers like Neal Moritz (*The Fast and the Furious*) and Stacey Sher (*Erin Brockovich*), and execs like Robert Greenblatt (*Showtime *president). If you get in, go.*

movie protagonists (Atticus Finch, Peter Parker, Clarice Starling, Rubin "Hurricane" Carter . . .). Coincidence? We think not.

Now stop. Put down your headset. It's time to spice things up a little. Did the indy script that your cousin's best friend wrote make you cry? Then stop sitting on it and go tell your producer boss that he must read it. The boss said it was "too small"? Make 40 more copies and start sending it to every drink, breakfast, and hookup you've had in the last year. Having a strong opinion, regardless of whether people agree with it, will gain you respect as someone who *is* strong. Especially when David Fincher signs on to direct your script as his next movie. Besides, at least you *have* a point of view, which is actually hard to find in a town of people-pleasers.

"But I want to *be* David Fincher, not produce for him." Okay. Then go shoot a scene on the cheap, edit that puppy to perfection, and shop for funding for the entire movie. "Too much of a crapshoot. Maybe I want to be a talent agent." Then go to every actors showcase. You're bound to find one star in the making. "Development's too slow. I want to run a marketing division instead." Write up a business plan on how to reach a grassroots audience for your company's next slasher flick.

Whatever you decide you want to do, just get out there and put those brilliant ideas to work. Pretty soon Paul-Newman-spaghetti-boy will be stuck in his low-rung executive job and you'll be running the company. Seriously, don't let us down. We're counting on you to buy our screenplays someday.

P.S. Please, don't go telling all of your little friends this one. It's a gem, so you should just savor it. After all, not everyone can be a force of nature. Do that and we'll have an industry implosion on our hands.

EXAMPLES OF SHEER WILL POWER:

- **Sidney Poitier.** As a black actor in a racist industry and era, he worked menial jobs during the day and studied acting at night before getting cast in his first Broadway play. That led to a string of film roles and eventually becoming the first African American to win the Best Actor Oscar. That wasn't enough, though. He became a director, ambassador, and knight too. This is what it means to be an iconoclast.

- **George Lucas.** First he started a film company with Francis Ford Coppola (American Zoetrope) so he could make movies outside the confines of the studio system. After much success, he decided to make a movie that relied entirely on technology that didn't exist. So he invented the technology. Bazillions of dollars later, we are jealous.

- **Lucille Ball.** After being fired time and time again as a stage actress, she persevered to become the Queen of the B's (as in B movies). Her radio show for CBS led to *I Love Lucy*. Although the executives were reluctant to cast Desi Arnaz, Ball insisted and the show became the gem that we all know and love. The couple didn't stop there though. They founded their own studio (Desilu), which became home to some of the most successful TV series in history (*Star Trek, The Andy GriffithShow,* and *Mission: Impossible*). Way to stick to your guns, lady.

- **Spike Lee.** Outspoken and underrated, Mr. Lee showed up every fellow NYU film student in his graduating class. First he directed *She's Gotta Have It* for little dough. When that became a hit, he was signed to direct commercials for Nike (Air Jordan anyone?). Many indy *and* studio movies later, he continues to voice his strong, and often controversial, beliefs.

- **Salma Hayek.** Famous for stripping with a snake at one point, she demanded to be known as more than a bombshell by starting her own production company. The Oscar-nominated *Frida* followed, which led to her directing the Emmy Award–winning *The Maldonado Miracle* and, finally, to producing the hit series *Ugly Betty*.

- **Ari Emanuel.** This head of the Endeavor Agency (and the basis for the Ari Gold character on *Entourage*) began his career in the mailroom of CAA before becoming an agent at ICM. In 1995 he and his old buds from the mailroom founded Endeavor, which now ranks as one of Hollywood's top agencies. It pays to be a power-hungry agent. Just try not to abuse your assistant while you're at it.

- **Melvin Van Peebles.** The forefather of independent cinema. Fed up with not seeing realistic portrayals of black people on-screen, he made his first film, *The Story of a Three-Day Pass,* about a black soldier, which got him a contract with Columbia Pictures. After working on studio movies, he directed and starred in *Sweet Sweetback's Baadassssss Song,* a script that no studio would fund, with his own money. The result? The start of the blaxploitation movement. (See son Mario's 2004 film *BAADASSSSS!* to learn more about this revolutionary.)

- **Robert Rodriguez.** In order to fund *El Mariachi,* this director volunteered for medical research studies. Using innovative, guerrilla-style directing techniques, the film became a hit and led him to make ground-breaking, moneymaking films like *Desperado, Sin City,* and *Spy Kids*. It just takes a good idea, a camera, and some gumption, folks. We all love some gumption, but remember that a brilliant director's mind doesn't hurt either.

- **George Clooney.** From cheesy sitcom actor to Hollywood royalty, the dude never saw the sky's limits. Instead he had the foresight to walk away from *ER* (and tons of cash) and join forces with Steven Soderbergh (the new Steven Spielberg). Together they made movies like *Oceans 11, 12, 13 . . .* , *Good Night and Good Luck,* and *Syriana*.

- **Steve Kloves.** He was an unpaid intern for a Hollywood agent when he gained attention for his first screenplay. He's now known as the *Harry Potter* screenwriter. The lesson? Be the "squeaky wheel" intern, not the "great photocopier" intern.

- **Michael Arndt.** This *Little Miss Sunshine* writer (and Best Screenplay winner) was Matthew Broderick's assistant for years before he quit to write. See? Dreams really do come true.

TRUE CONFESSIONS

"Everyone told me it was all about getting my foot in the door at a great production company. So I was thrilled when a job for a junior exec fell into my lap. I decided from the get-go I would work longer and harder than everyone else in order to set myself apart from the crowd. I'd shadow my boss and do whatever she did. Only problem was, about four weeks into the job, I realized most of what she did consisted of long-winded phone calls about her extensive wedding planning and troubled breakups. How'd she get the job in the first place? Through the grapevine I heard she was quite the promiscuous networker. Yeah, *that* way. Since then she just coasted under the radar. Meanwhile I spent the day doing her notes and adding calls to the phone sheet that would never be returned while she chatted incessantly about floral arrangements and thermographed invitations. When her contract came to an end the bosses decided she'd be better at producing weddings, not movies. So, with the company now in need of a new C.E., I walked into the president's office and handed over all my notes, coverage, and scene breakdowns that I'd done over the past year. The next day I got promoted. I should drop the old boss a note thanking her for making me do her job all that time." **—A.M.**

Beware the Words "Thank You"

"Will you please tighten my golden handcuffs?"

HOLLYWOOD TYPES HAVE LITTLE TROUBLE manipulating their assistants to do whatever their blackened hearts desire. That's because you'll submit to anything if you believe it will bring you closer to that pot of gold called a promotion. In return, you will receive little to nothing. No thank you, no pat on the back, no blue ribbon. You will simply get more work. Sigh. There will be one time, however, let's say eight to ten months into your new job, when you'll be going about your own business, busting your ass to prepare your boss's Cobb salad while answering phones and yelling at interns when it'll happen. The trap.

"Hey sport, I just wanted to tell you, I really appreciate everything you do. Really. It means a lot to me."

And it's at this moment that your heart will stop. You'll look up at the sky to see if the heavens have parted. You'll wonder, "Did that Vicodin I took last weekend finally kick in, because either I'm hallucinating or my boss was actually cool for once." None of the above. What's more likely is that your boss, sensing a mental breakdown on your part, knew he had to act quick if he was going to keep you from storming out the door shouting, "I quit this lousy job, you stinking stupid worthless excuse for a blah blah blah . . ." So he thanked you, and for the first time in a long time, you liked your job. You felt validated and needed. In other words, you walked right into the trap.

It's a dirty little secret among bosses in Tinseltown that the key to keeping an assistant handcuffed to the cube is to withhold love for as long as possible. We've tried to resist falling victim to the thank-you voodoo, but it's hard. We assistants have come to believe that cruelty and insanity are as normal a part of the workplace as they are in an abusive relationship. Gratitude, though? Public acknowledgment?? God, what did we do to deserve such good luck??!

Don't fall for it. From this point on the words "thank you" have just the same effect as "screw you." You are a cold, indifferent machine of an assistant, impervious to emotional manipulation. The people who do not follow our advice will get sucked in deep—way beyond a level that is healthy—and end up thinking that this crappy-ass job is all they're cut out for. The result? They become lifers.

OTHER TRAPS TO AVOID:

Believe you me, bosses have many other tricks up their sleeves beside the well-timed "thank you." Look out for these additional, potentially fatal traps.

Boss says: "You're doing such a great job that I convinced H.R. to give you a salary bump."
Translation: I think you're a sucker whose soul can be bought for an extra $50 a week.

Boss says: "Why don't you take those premiere tix on my desk? Leave at seven if you need to."
Translation: That movie sucks and I have therapy at seven, so take the tix and we'll pretend I actually like you.

Boss says: "Order me the squab from L'Orangerie and feel free to get whatever you want."
Translation: The company pays for lunch, I don't want to watch you drool over my $50 plate of pigeon, and you're too stupid to put two and two together.

Boss says: "You look great today."
Translation: I think you're insecure and this simple lie/compliment will make up for the ridicule I'm about to inflict on you.

Boss says: "Why don't you take a few days off?"
Translation: I need to interview for your replacement while you're out.

Boss says: "You really make me look better."
Translation: You matter only because I matter.

Boss says: "You do your job so much better than I ever could."
Translation: You are so pathetic and I'm not.

Boss says: "You're promoted. We're just figuring out how soon we can make it official."
Translation: We can't afford to promote you, but we're going to pretend like we can in order to keep you as my assistant for the next 14 years.

Boss says: "I think you're ready to move on to other things."
Translation: You're fired.

Make Them Show You the Money

"There's something I need you to do for me. Increase my salary by 150 percent."

YOU HAVE AMAZING MANNERS. YOUR PARENTS raised you to say please and thank you. You help old women cross the street. You, my friend, are goodness incarnate.

That would also explain why you never ask for anything at work. When your company has a premiere, you don't ask for an invite. While the other assistants go out for lunch every Friday, you stay in for fear of putting out your boss. When your boss checked "satisfactory" in the work ethic box during your evaluation, you didn't ask why. Instead you kept your nose to the grindstone and told yourself you'd just try a little harder even though deep down you knew you were the hardest working person in showbiz.

Wrong.

If there's anything working in the Biz has taught us, it's to ask for what you want. Think about it. Did Tom Hanks end up getting paid $20 million per picture because he was polite? Hell no, it's because the dude—and his agent—knew he was worth it and thus demanded it. Good thing his box-office tally proved them right. Did Stacey Snider become the head of Universal (and then DreamWorks) because she waited for her time in the sun to come along? Ha! She took that job and ran with it, becoming one of the most powerful people in town.

★ *Call the shots like Cruise.*

Look at the successful people in this business and you will find that they have one thing in common—they are askers. For example, say you're the CEO of a major studio and you need to choose a new chairman. In office 1 you have the diligent and steady Nice Guy. He handles all his movies with aplomb, the actors appreciate his honesty, and he'll never embarrass you in a staff meeting. Now office 2 tells a different story. Ball Buster is notorious for her temper tantrums on the set, she bulldozes over her competition, and she's not afraid of making harsh demands—even if that means getting Julia Roberts to cut her fee. Do you even have to ask whom the CEO will choose? Every studio needs its own Ball Buster to succeed. And do you know what else? She'll probably ask for triple her current salary. Now you know how she can afford Cher's old mansion on the PCH.

As an assistant, even when you've proven your competence, you might find it harder to ask for things. Stop it right now. If you don't get yourself noticed, no one will notice you. It's that simple. Think you deserve a raise? March into your boss's office and have ten reasons to justify why. Want to sit in on a pitch? Manipulate his emotions so he feels bad not having already invited you. Just don't, and we can't stress this enough, sit back and wait for the good karma to come your way. Make your own karma.

OTHER POINTERS TO GET THE RAISE YOU DESERVE:

We know you make only 0.00001 percent of Reese Witherspoon's going rate, but the fact remains that the corporation isn't dying to throw you more dough. Here are some tips to get what you deserve.

- **Don't be nervous.** If you find yourself sweating, quickly change the topic to something innocuous like the schedule or the phone sheet. Only when cool (and dry) should you bring up the raise.

- **Speak with authority.** Approach your boss's desk like OJ's lawyer, the late Johnny Cochran, would approach the bench—that is, with such a convincing argument that she can't say no.

- **Have your ducks in a row.** Write your arguments down on an index card, memorize them, and be able to list them off at the drop of that hat. Just don't bring these refresher notes into the meeting. You don't want to seem like even *you* need help remembering why you deserve the raise.

- **Incentivize your boss.** Offer up actual, concrete ways in which her life will get better as a result of the raise. "I'll get to work a half hour earlier, answer your weekend calls within two hours, and be a happier employee overall." Just make sure you can deliver.

Have a Plan B. There's a good chance the boss is going to say no. Be prepared when he does, whether that means giving your notice, accepting your current salary, or forgetting to order his wife flowers on their anniversary, you passive-aggressive little . . .

Bury the Hatchet in the Name of Good Business

"You will never work in this town again!"

YOU'RE GOING TO MAKE A LOT OF ENEMIES IN your new line of work. Trust us, no matter how nice you think you are or how strong your conscience is, you will screw someone over.

Backstabbing, after all, makes Hollyworld go round. Intentional or not, you will find yourself in situations where you won't be able to help yourself from wielding the knife. "Is it really that bad for me to tell the boss that Jake expenses his personal meals if that means I'll get the promotion over him?" And down the rabbit hole you go. Beware though—you might end up on the receiving end of that knife too.

"Et tu, Bridgette??"

Yup, it seems that Bridgette, the sweet little intern you trusted with all your secrets, was not so sweet after all. Maybe she brought you those yummy carrot muffins every morning, but she didn't think twice about stabbing you in the back. You see, it doesn't matter how or when it happens. There will come a point where the people nearest and dearest to you will screw you over. What will subsequently grow inside of you is a huge, viral-spreading, soul-eating grudge. For the rest of your Hollywood career you will fear seeing this person at a party—not because she scares you, but rather because you're scared of what you're going to do to her.

Take a deep breath now. Because just as it's inevitable that starlets end up in rehab, it's also inevitable that you will be forced to work with your archenemy one day. Maybe you'll be a studio executive who

wants to buy a genius spec titled *Mosquito* (think *Jaws* with more itching), but the producer is the same sweetie pie who stole your promotion back in '02. Or maybe you'll be an agent looking for new talent when you find out your ex-boyfriend is taking meetings with all the big agencies after winning the Best New

Actor award at the Toronto Film Festival. Do you refuse to buy this spec or meet with the actor? Hell no.

People, you must put aside all of your personal vendettas, crosses to bear, and elaborate schemes to enact vengeance when it comes to your professional life. Why? Because in Tinseltown, business comes before pleasure. You'd be stupid to let a ripe business opportunity pass you by because of some little incident back in the mailroom a dozen years ago. So put aside the grudge and make your enemy your frenemy. Now we're not saying you have to actually forgive your frenemy; just *act* as if you have. Only then will you have mastered the fine movie-business art that we like to call "Making Craploads of Cash."

TRUE CONFESSIONS

"She worked in our mailroom for three to four months tops. It wasn't that we didn't like her, just that you could tell—she thought she was too smart to be there. When she got fired (for telling a partner his star client didn't deserve his seven-figure paycheck), I never expected to hear about her again. But then it started floating around town, this screenplay she had written about all the people at our company. She didn't even try to mask who was who. Like if the scene was about an agent named Rich, she'd change the name to Rick, that sort of thing. The fact that she made the characters all seem like the worst people on the planet— exposing details about affairs, doing drugs in the ladies' room, talking shit about their clients—didn't help. We all knew what she was doing. It was revenge, pure and simple. The poor thing just didn't realize that you can't bite the hand that feeds you— especially in Hollywood. The last I heard she moved to New York to get into publishing. I'm guessing that's not gonna work out either once everyone catches wind of her mean ol' mouth." **—K.L.**

Fail Up

COME CLOSER. NO, CLOSER. YOU DON'T WANT THE REST OF YOUR coworkers to hear this, do you? Because this tidbit is the one you've been waiting for—the BIG SECRET that will fast track you to success. Okay, here we go now. Remember, don't tell anyone.

Screw up.

"I'm sorry. Did you say, 'SCREW UP'?"

Yes, we said screw up. Mess up. Err. In other words, *don't be too good at your job.* We know, this is hard for you to swallow. All the other lessons have taught you how to be the perfect little assistant and now here we come, pretty much telling you to sabotage yourself.

Great assistants in Hollywood do not automatically make great HPPs (whether that's as an agent, producer, studio chief, marketing guru, etc.). In fact, the greatest assistants are usually the ones that stay just that—assistants. Why would a boss promote an assistant when it will be impossible to find a replacement to do as good a job? It'd be easier to promote someone *else's* assistant than to lose you. They think, "How will I explain to this new person, this stranger, that I have herpes and they need to pick up my prescription every Saturday? And isn't this new person going to want a promotion too, eventually? How annoying!"

As a human, you only have a limited amount of energy. If you're putting all of it into being a great assistant, you won't have any left over to read scripts, do notes, or polish your pitching skills—all the things you'll need to do in order to be promoted. Hence, there's only one way to give your boss the incentive to promote you and that, my friends, is to make mistakes. Now, let's be crystal clear: not mistakes that will have a lasting impact on your boss's job or his personal life (calling the wife by the mistress's name, for example) but little, annoying ones. Some examples: Forgetting to order her favorite sparkling water, spilling salad dressing on the carpet, or using the trades to clean up the dog's accident before your boss has had a chance to read them.

"Won't he just fire me?"

Well that's a definite possibility. But this is why we recommend that you start screwing up only once you've proven that you're a hard worker and a good—not great—assistant. But now you've started making little boo-boos here and there. You forget things. You show just a teensy-weensy amount of attitude when he asks you to do personal stuff. And now the boss is annoyed. So annoyed that he has only one option: to promote you. And you'll cry tears of joy when it happens.

SCREW UP OR MAJOR F-UP? A QUIZ:

Which of the below qualify as healthy screwups—meaning, you won't get fired but instead pushed up the ladder? It's a fine line, kiddos; learn how to walk it.

1. You forgot to pick up his tuxedo from dry cleaning right before the Oscars.

2. You dropped a call from George Lucas.

3. You forgot to add pepperoni to the pizza order.

4. You showed up a half hour late this morning.

5. You talked back to her husband.

6. You broke his favorite coffee mug.

7. You are three months behind on expenses.

8. You read a script at lunch instead of filling her gas tank.

9. You left the office early because you thought he was already in his screening.

10. You sent a company-wide e-mail about your boss's weight that was meant only for her dietician.

Answers: 3, 4, 6, 7, 8, 9. The rest are big bad boo-boos and don't come crying to us if you commit them.

Great Ideas Aren't Cheap

"I really loved your thoughts on the script. Why don't you write them up and throw them on a memo for me?"

GREAT! SO YOU CAN "THROW" *YOUR* NAME ON them and pretend they're from you? Super! I'll get right on that.

This is a tricky one. In order to get to the next phase of your career there's a basic rule in Hollywood: do the job above you. If you're aiming to be an agent, scour the streets for new actors and pore over the scripts for the up-and-coming writers. If you want to produce, bring your neighbor the director together with your coworker the writer and, voilà, you are producing. If it's the studio gig you want, then take home the **weekend read** and do notes just for fun. Yes, you're going to have to do your job and your boss's in order to prove that you are ready for the promotion. Sleeping? That's for pansies.

There's a second part to this lesson though: how to get credit for doing the job above you. There's no point in staying up all night doing a **scene breakdown** on *Batman Returns: Again* if nobody knows you're doing it. When doing the extra work—whatever industry you're working in—make sure you let your work be seen. You put in the time, now strut your stuff. That means e-mailing a copy of your script notes to the boss, or asking if it's okay for you to give them to the head of the company, or keeping a copy in your "portfolio" to show potential employers you know how to write good notes.

Beware, though: There may come a time when your boss will steal one of your ideas. No, not all bosses do this, but there are definitely some who do, and you're going to want to be on the lookout for them. Say you think of a genius remake idea. You do an extensive search and find out that the rights are now owned by the almost-dead maid of the original rights' holder. Armed with this information you barge into Boss's office: "Eureka, eureka! I found it, the studio's next summer blockbuster." And wouldn't you know it? Your boss agrees with you—and then passes off the information as his own. Before you know it, the studio is offering the cheat a promotion and a raise, while you're still organizing the files from his 1981 divorce. This is a case when you've done the job above you so well that you're a threat. You go home that night crying into your pillow. "Now I know how Melanie Griffith felt! I'm living her tragedy!"

Hold on, sister. There's no crying in Hollyball. Melanie figured out how to snag the corner office, and you will too. The hard truth: Chances are this brilliant idea you've come up with was a fluke, a kind of creative Halley's Comet. So rather than wait for the next one, tell Big Shot it's confession time or you're going to send a mass e-mail to the company stating exactly what happened. You've even kept all those e-mails to the maid, right? Perfect, because no one is going to believe you unless you have evidence.

P.S. Obviously, pick your battles carefully (refer back to Rule 47, "Norma Rae," p. 110, for a refresher), but when you do something great, you best bloody well stand up for yourself.

★ *Climb to the top . . .*
of all that paperwork.

Surround Yourself with Good People

"I know she's bad for me, but I'm hooked, man. She's got a power I can't explain . . ."

AS AN ASSISTANT TO HOLLYWOOD'S WHO'S WHO you've gotten an up-close-and-personal view of what success in the Biz truly means. Sure there's the corner office in Bev Hills, the dinner parties with celebs, and the expense account at Matsuhisa,* but by our calculations your boss is only about 18 percent happy. The other 82 percent? That's made up of varying amounts of fatigue, anger, resentment, greed, and jealousy. Of course this is only your average HPP. Some feel worse.

"Are you saying that money does not buy happiness??" Yes.

There are some execs in the Biz who break the misery mold. They are happy even, leading balanced lives and finding fulfillment in their work. "Who are these people and how do I find them?" Look around. Does the exec across the hall leave the office early every Friday to spend time with her kids? Did the producer at your company buy all the assistants lunch after winning Best Picture? Does the director that you're P.A.ing for make it a point to laugh at least once a day? Yes, these are those atypical bosses who, if not happy all the time, at least strive to be. You won't find these types often, but once you do, you must *never* let them out of your sight. These folks are *rare*. From here on out this person is your American Idol, Action Hero, and Savior all wrapped into one. In other words, this is who you want to be.

Really, we can't stress this one enough. In order to find both success and happiness in Holly-woe-is-me, you must find people who already have both. Otherwise you're headed down the Path to Hell with no yellow brick road in sight, my friends.

For example, say you want to be an agent. Now look around you again. Is there an agent in your halls whom you would want to be? Or do they all seem rather unstable? Psychotic even? To the point where the only thing that seems to lift their spirits is flicking rubber bands at you? If it's the latter, you might want to reconsider the Agent Trainee Program you're applying for.

A go-to place for both young and old Hollywood, Matsuhisa is sushi for the stars (it's the same owner as Nobu, after all). Don't be surprised to see Bruce Willis and his new girlfriend having sashimi at one table while his newly legal daughters down sake across the room (129 N. La Cienega Blvd., Beverly Hills; 310-659-9639).

"But I won't be like that! I'll work hard and still have time for my family."

Wow. You almost made us laugh. If we only had a nickel for all the times your evil boss said those exact words back in the day. If you really want to avoid becoming like Dr. Evil, ban the bad people from your life. That includes fellow assistants, friends, and, yes, even family members who are a bad influence. We know it's hard, but cleaning all the Negative Nancy's out of your house will free up space for all the good influences. Only then will you experience the state of nirvana known as a "healthy relationship."

"When I moved to L.A. everyone warned me how mean and crazy and vindictive the people would be. Especially bosses. Not her, though. In my interview she made *me* a coffee. On my first day she took me to lunch at the Ivy—'to bond.' By the second month we were getting manis and pedis every Tuesday, and that was only after shopping for shoes at Barneys (that she would buy). I hit the jackpot. Really, she was the nicest, smartest, and most encouraging boss a girl could ever hope for. There was only one problem. Even though she kept putting me up for better jobs all over town, the thought of leaving her always made me sad. I loved working for her. A little too much. She was the one who finally said it: 'You're too smart to be my assistant forever. I'm giving you four weeks to find another job. After that you're fired.' She stuck to her word, too (as usual). It didn't matter though. Getting fired was the best thing that ever happened to me. Now I'm a C.E. at [bleep] and just got an associate producer credit on my first movie. I do miss her, though. And those shoes." **—I.C.**

TRUE CONFESSIONS

Work Your Magic Behind the Curtain

NOW YOU'LL NEVER FIND AN EXECUTIVE WHO WILL ADMIT TO WHAT we're about to tell you. No, because by doing so he would draw attention to the fact that he is expendable. The truth? The bosses don't run Hollywood. You do.

Of course, you're wondering why your paycheck doesn't reflect this. Details, details. The fact remains that you wield more power than you think, and that's because you are young. And your boss, well, is not.

This business thrives on youth. Whether it's the teenage boys flocking to Adam Sandler movies, the teenage girls crowning the Olsen twins as fashion icons, or the young bloggers deciding who's the next James Dean, the predilections of the young mean influence, influence means power, and power means $$. Lots and lots of $$.

One of the most desirable, coveted qualities in the movie business is originality. (We know, you wouldn't know it from the number of awful, predictable, derivative movies coming out. But let's save that discussion for our next book.) Who's more effortlessly original than young people? They see things in a way that no one else does, and every executive in town is fiending for their creative ideas. Guess what? Assistants are the conduit between the two groups. You are the only ones who have both your hands in the business of movies and your fingers on the pulse and passions of youth. Bosses have no choice but to rely on their assistants to tell them who's the next hot director, up-and-coming comic, and pop star who is ripe to become a film star.

How you take advantage of this is simple: Become your boss's Culture Coach. Provide her with a unique service called "keeping your boss in the know." Educate her on what's hip, trendy, street. Save her from her own stale instincts. If she's thinking of paying $20 mil to cast an A-list movie star, mention that a cheaper, up-and-coming alternative might make the movie more interesting. If she needs a fresh song for a kung fu gang movie, slip the music supervisor the CD of the punk band you saw at Spaceland last Thursday. Pretty soon you'll be known as the kid with great taste, which is way better than "the assistant who makes great coffee." Then what? Get ready to be promoted. You've got loads of culture just pumping out of you, so use it to get ahead.

THE ETIQUETTE OF SHOWING OFF TO THE BOSS:

Like that lesson about asking for a raise, showing off is all about timing, people. So if your boss just got off a call and is in the middle of composing a crucial e-mail to the head of the studio, this is not the time to explain why Sandra Oh would be an offbeat choice in that art film you can't cast. Here are some good spots to impress the boss:

1. The hall. Walk your boss to a meeting. Tell him you're going to go over updates and then pepper your brilliant ideas into the conversation. "You have a 2:30 notes call with the director, who by the way, really needs to cut down on the grotesque T&A shots if he wants any sane women under 35 to go to his film." Please though, do not display diarrhea of the mouth. There's no need to listen to yourself speak. You should know what you sound like by now.

2. The car. Drive your boss to lunch or to the airport or to the beach house in the 'Bu. There's nothing like a quiet enclosed space to prove your genius.

3. The post-favor. Did you kindly buy your boss a latte on your way into work this morning? What a great time to get her to scratch your back too. "That reminds me, I wrote up this market analysis on why it's better to advertise on YouTube than on TV."

4. The memo. If you can't ever get a minute alone with the boss, write up a memo and staple it to the front page of the script you know he's going to look at tonight.

5. The hold. You're both on hold with the super busy agent so you take this moment to share your opinion on the new shooting draft of the Harrison Ford flick . . . OKAY, THAT WAS A TEST. In no way should you ever share your opinion while on hold. (As discussed in Rule 22, "The Conversation.")

Sometimes It's Okay to Cheat

SOMEONE ON YOUR TRACKING BOARD JUST TOLD YOU ABOUT A NEW job. Maybe it's an assistant gig at a studio, a story editor position at Imagine, or a part in the Las Vegas showgirl revue you've always obsessed about. Point is, you really want to go for the interview. Your friend's sister's college roommate is doing the hiring, so you're a shoo-in. But then it comes. That overwhelming, sinking feeling known as guilt. You feel bad going behind your boss's back. So bad that you even consider bailing on the interview.

Oh, jeez, here we go again. Remember that "All About Eve" rule on page 93? How, when all is said and done, you have to worry about one person and one person only—yourself. Good, now this is one of those times when you have to put that lesson into action. That means that you will in no way miss out on this interview. Not sure if you even want the job? Still go. You must use the interview to find out if you do.

"Okay, fine. But how do I get the two hours off from work? Should I just tell her the truth?" Hold up there, killer. Now, we're all for telling the truth and all (see Rule 44, "Pinocchio," for example), but you have to be very, very careful about this one. The way we see it, the only time it's worth telling your boss that you're going for an interview is when you can 100 percent guarantee her support. If there's even a 1 percent chance she's going to (1) be jealous and/or (2) sabotage your chances of getting the job and/or (3) fire you from your current job—you must take precautions. In an ideal world this would mean telling her way ahead of time that you have a doctor's appointment or jury duty. Hell, take the whole day off while you're at it.

P.S. Don't wear your interview outfit to work, lest you raise the suspicions of every receptionist and executive in the office. Yes, your taupe powersuit is a red flag. Do a quick change in the car instead. Otherwise, you'll be impressed how quickly your boss managed to clear out your desk by the time you're back. And you don't want to pack while wearing your Sunday's best.

HELPFUL HINTS TO HELP YOU
SCORE THAT NEXT JOB:

Like a hot spec script, you too can be at the receiving end of a bidding war. Simply follow the three steps below and you could be running the studio by 30.

- **Sell, sell, sell.** Self-promotion is an art form. Oversell and you are a braggart; undersell and you won't get noticed. Hence, be subtle about the way you talk about your accomplishments. Drop hints— not bombs—about your roommate's script that you helped develop before it sold to Paramount. Talk about how you were the one to recommend *The Da Vinci Code* as a possible film, but only when the movie comes up in conversation.

- **Play hard to get.** You will become infinitely more attractive to a potential employer if you have another job offer. Say Miramax offers you a job right there in the room. Don't say yes. Instead, tell them, "I have another offer. Can I think about it?" Now watch as they do cartwheels in an attempt to hire you. (Don't worry—they don't need to know that your other offer is to run the patchwork division in your aunt's knitting store.)

- **Don't tell the whole story.** There is such a thing as Too Much Information. Hence, we recommend divulging only half your story. For instance, did you produce a short that won Slamdance and are now shopping the feature rights? Say, "I can't go into the details but I'm in negotiations for a new project." That's all. Like a good movie, people will be all the more intrigued if you leave them wanting more.

RULE #80: Basic Instinct

Go with Your Gut

YOU GOT THE PROMOTION?! OH MY GOD! WE'RE SO PROUD OF YOU!! Truly. But now comes the hard part—making a decision. It seems like just yesterday you felt trapped in your job with no light at the end of the tunnel and the next day you're overwhelmed with the options laid out in front of you.

You've been offered a job to head the film division of a new media company and another one to go work for the A-list producer whose assistant is guaranteed an associate producer credit on his next movie. And let's not forget the one you already turned down—to go work as the junior partner to the agent starting his own management company. Boy, our little baby's all grown up!

Well, we also know that it's at times like these when you will feel overwhelmed. You'll probably turn to your fellow colleagues for career advice. You'll want to know what each and every person thinks about your potential new boss and company. Only then will you be able to make an informed decision about which job will most greatly benefit your future. Wrong!

We are strong believers that the key to surviving in this business is learning how to trust your gut. That's how you'll decide which scripts you like, what actors to cast, and how big a budget to give that movie you know won't make as much money as the director thinks. Your gut is really the only weapon you have in Hollywar.

Take your decision about your next job as a for instance. Because L.A. is such a small world, everyone you know will have something to say about your new boss or company. You'll get such a wide range of opinions that you'll be in assisted living by the time you make a decision. For example, you're thinking about taking a job as a junior exec at a production company famous for making Oscar-caliber movies like *Kangaroo Killers 7: Marsupial Mass Murder.* Everyone says, "Turn it down." But you have a good feeling about the place. They've hired you to upgrade their slate and even though the pay is paltry, you think you can make this work to your advantage. You'll make this slate your own and turn this fledgling company into the next Imagine. First up, your screenwriter girlfriend's riveting script about a clown, trapeze artist, and snake who must hitchhike across Utah in order to catch up with the circus that left them behind. Romantic feelings and dramatic fall-out ensue. (Boy, we always knew you had good taste!)

Take the job. Only you know what your gut is saying. And only listening to it—and making mistakes based on it—will prepare you for being an HPP.

Celebrate the Small Victories

"Oh god, what if I say something wrong in the first weekend read meeting?"

WE GET IT. YOU'RE NERVOUS. TERRIFIED EVEN. You feel unprepared for your new job, like they made a mistake when they hired you or that it's a big practical joke. Wow, you really *are* like us— stressed, neurotic, and a bit crazy. Sorry about that.

Listen up, kids—this one's important: There aren't going to be that many good days in your life as a Hollywood assistant. Experience tells us that people in the Biz rarely take time to feel happy about their accomplishments. If an actor wins the Best Supporting Oscar, for example, he's on the phone with his agent the following day, asking where the next part is. If a studio opens its animated movie at number one, they're hurrying to put together the sequel before the weekend is over.

"I'm not going to be like that, thanks." That's right! Because instead you're going to take a moment to enjoy the victories—big and small. We'd even recommend a whole month if you can manage it. Treat yourself to dinner at Boa, rent out the Buffalo Club for a private party, or take that long-dreamt-of three-week backpacking trek through the mountains of Burma. "But I'm taking a pay cut." Oh well, then just park a keg of Natty Light in your apartment's bathtub and throw the most hip-happening "I Rock!" celebration that Beverlywood has ever seen. Here are some more ideas on how to enjoy the moment:

1. **Buy something.** Is there a pair of shoes you're craving? A High Definition TV you love? Go on, spoil yourself.

2. **Pamper yourself.** Massages, facials, seaweed wraps. These are all appropriate ways to rejoice.

3. **Spread the wealth.** Take your intern out to lunch. Send your mom an "I was thinking of you" card. Write a check to the Red Cross. It's much more fun sharing your good tidings than keeping them all to your lonesome.

4. **Take the day off.** Work is hard. So forget about it for a day and go for a drive to San Diego along the PCH. It's not quite a road trip, but will still feel great.

Pick an Egg Already

"I don't know really. I guess I want to be a producer. But screenwriting's really interesting to me too. And then of course I hope to direct eventually. But this vice president of Home Video job is fine for now."

CAN WE BE COMPLETELY HONEST WITH YOU? Seriously, there's something we need to get off our chest. Some of you drive us crazy. You're ready to leave your job—we get that. But one day you're talking about how you want to be an agent and the next it's directing and the day after that it's costume design. Make a decision already! Because unless you're the second coming of Leonardo da Vinci, chances are your genius is limited to one field. Only a few people in the history of the Biz have triumphed in several arenas (Orson Welles, Jodie Foster, Keenan Ivory Wayans), and none of them *started out* doing everything. No, they began their career as one thing (actor) and only once they mastered this one thing did they move on to the next (director). The same goes for you.

"But I don't know what I want to do!"

Big deal; ask a few 80-year-olds and they'll probably say the same thing. The trick at this point is to pretend like you know what you want to do. All you really have to worry about is today. Right now, in this moment, what part of the Biz do you want to pursue? Is it writing or directing? Casting or production design? If you're not sure, then flip a coin. "Seriously??" Yes.

Waffling's a big waste of time and energy. We know it's easy to get distracted, especially when you see your friends becoming successful in other fields ("If Leanne can be a cinematographer, then maybe *I* can be a cinematographer . . . And Marcie has that sweet gig in costume design . . . I always have good costumes"). This is only a trap. You have to trust that your time will come—as long as you stay focused.

That means referring back to your Wish List. We're not talking about your goals 20 years from now ("Build mahogany display case for Oscar, check . . ."). We're talking about your immediate goals. Since you are young and have your entire career in front of you, there's really no way to make a wrong decision right now. Even better is that you probably won't have that many options. There are only so many jobs that you can get from an assistant desk, so you might as well take the first one that tickles your fancy. So flip the coin. You'll be happy you did.

Know When to Quit

"Boss, we need to talk . . ."

PERHAPS THE SCARIEST SPECIMEN ROAMING the halls of Hollywood is what we call a **lifer.** Go to any agency, studio lot, or production office and you're bound to find her. She snaps at the guests, fills the void in her life with See's Candies, and is the first one to tell you how she would have handled that drama with the florist better. In other words, she's exactly the person you don't want to become—old, bitter, past her prime, and much too smart for this job.

So how does it happen that some assistants who started out with great big dreams of taking over the town wind up stuck in some crappy job with some crappy boss ten years later? Because they get too comfortable. Sure, they're friendly with A-list producers, get invited to the coolest holiday parties, and make a pretty good living. But they also have a job they loathe. Somewhere along the line, they started to believe that answering phones was their destiny. Oh, the humanity.

"Wow, that's me."

Then it's clear, the fat lady wants to sing. And by denying her that right—by staying in this job—you are accepting a future of middling success, second-class citizenship, and fits of depression. That's right, you are just too good for this job. And staying in it—whether it's for the paycheck, the perks, or your own fear—is not okay. So get up, walk into that schmo's office, and say two of the most powerful words in the language: "I quit!" But be mature about it, of course. We suggest: "I've learned so much from you and I really feel ready to move up to the next level." Or you could try: "I've thought long and hard about it and now want to learn about different areas of business." The point is to never make the reason for leaving about them. Try to be grateful for everything they taught you. Even the most difficult of jobs are learning opportunities—and for that you should be grateful.

So here comes the hard part—knowing when it's time to get the hell out of Dodge. Here are some telltale signs: If the first thing you'll think of in the morning is your boss. If your younger, peppier coworkers rarely talk to you. If your blood boils when you're called out on a mistake. If you yell at other assistants over the phone. If you can't remember how long you've worked at your current job. If you think about what you're going to have for lunch on your drive into the office each morning. If your old intern is now running Universal. If your desk is covered in photos of your cat. If you order cupcakes for people's half-birthdays just because it's, well, something to do . . . That's it! It's time to quit already.

RULE #84: St. Elmo's Fire

Build Bridges, Don't Torch Them

"Then I'm done! That's right jackass. I've been meaning to say this for a long time. You are truly one of the biggest, ugliest, meanest pieces of $%##!! ..."

EVERYONE KNOWS THAT YOU SHOULDN'T burn bridges. Actually heeding this advice is a different story. We know how tempting it can be. It's your last week on the job, your boss is totally picking on you, and you want to walk out that door screaming all your boss's deep dark secrets as you go. God, even just thinking about it gets us excited. But guess what? That's as far as it will go. Because this whole "I'm going to tell you exactly what I think of you" fantasy must stay just that—a fantasy. In other words, never tell off your boss.

"No fun!" Yeah, well this *is* your career we're talking about here. It's not meant to be fun. If we were talking about your personal life, then it'd be a whole different story. Yes, we think you should tell that girlfriend who cheated on you to "go die" or something. We agree, it's fine to stop responding to those e-mails from the friend who stole your entire Carly Simon box collection. And we wholeheartedly offer our support if you want to flick off the Hummer that just cut you off. However, we do not recommend that you do any of these things if these people work in the Biz.

Let us repeat ourselves: Tinseltown is a small town. Everyone knows everyone and the moment you piss off one person the tracking boards will be full of stories defaming you. This is especially true in Assistant World. After all, we are the ones with nonstop Internet access and blog addictions. Gossiping and backstabbing are pretty much what we're best at. It is precisely because of the incestuous nature of this industry, however, that you must always maintain a healthy distance from the feeling that we like to abbreviate as I.P.A.R.T.G.R.P.U. (I'm Pissed and Ready to Go Rough People Up).

People are going to tick you off. That's a given. Your boss is going to inspire thoughts of brutality and torture. Certain assistants will make your skin crawl. Even the interns are going to give you a case of "the rage." Still, it's the law of probability that some of the very people you hate will become wildly successful. If you're lucky, they'll forget why you two didn't like each other and the two of you will partner up to make a movie that takes Cannes by storm. How much better is this ending than the one where you told him off, he blackballed you, and you ended up eating beans for dinner every night outside your trailer in Chino?

Scared? Good, we knew that one would work.

BURN THAT BRIDGE! EXCEPTIONS TO THE RULE:

- **You are leaving the Biz forever.** (As in, "I'd rather change oil at Chevron than ever see a movie again, let alone have anything to do with making one.")

- **You were physically or mentally abused.** (As in, "It doesn't matter that I've burned a bridge because I've walked away with a kickass severance package.")

- **You know something that could ruin someone's career.** (As in, "If she tries to screw me over in the future I'll just post those scandalous photos from Cabo on Defamer.")

- **You will experience nirvana.** (As in, "By telling him off I'll reach levels of bliss that even the Dalai Lama will envy." By the way, this has never happened.)

Nothing else—and we mean nothing—will justify such foolish behavior.

Look Back Fondly

IT'S YOUR LAST DAY OF WORK BEFORE CLIMBING TO THE NEXT rung of your fabulous career and nothing would make you happier than to do cartwheels out the door. You won't do this. No, you are going to take a moment to reflect on everything you've learned.

Looking back on your time as an assistant may not be what you feel like doing right now. Maybe you'll see only the bad times—that "errand" to the Fresno County jail you had to run, how Janelle blamed you for that smell emanating from the men's bathroom, or when the boss made you dress up in that Little Bo Peep costume in front of the CEO.

Now that you're almost out of your job you have to take this opportunity to recall the good in the people and places you've spent the last few months or years. After all, they did teach you everything you know—how to negotiate a good back-end, why it's important to have a tough skin, where to find the tastiest lobster bisque . . . In the end, you'd be nothing without them, and only by showing your appreciation will you be able to plant the seeds that grow into future relationships.

Hence, here are some ideas on how to turn the contacts at your current job—bosses and fellow assistants alike—into relationships that will last a lifetime.

1. Write good-bye notes. There's nothing that says "thank you" like a real, handwritten note. Chances are it will end up in their desk drawer and they'll pull it out a year later, fondly remembering you as a sweet gem of a human, not the snake who selfishly left the company.

2. Over-sentimentalize. We're not saying you should cry at your good-bye bash, but it can't hurt to feel nostalgic about your time at the job. Laugh over the memories. You'll be surprised how many good ones there really are.

3. Remember that you owe them for your success. You'd never get anywhere in this world without others helping you get there. So go, tell your coworkers how much you appreciate their support. Ten years from now they'll go, "Oh, I remember Brian way back before he knew how to roll a call. Now he's running Columbia! It couldn't have happened to a more deserving guy."

4. Keep in touch. This is the most important one. As soon as you leave that door you'll be out of sight and mind. The way to make the most of your old contacts is to drop a random e-mail every so often. Send a link of the article about their favorite author or invite them to your birthday party in Venice that you know they'll never come to. Just stay in touch.

Be a Good Soul

"I won't ever expense my personal dinners. Scout's honor."

WE CAN HARDLY BELIEVE IT! IT SEEMS THAT just days ago you were a naïve college grad who didn't even know what "left word" meant (if you forgot already shame on you. Turn back to Rule 21) and now look at you—you're a seasoned assistant who knows that neither Barney Greengrass nor William Morris are living, breathing people. "Are we finally done?" Not so fast, young pup. There is a final lesson to be learned: *being a good person.*

As young people starting a career we often feel put upon. Maniacal boss? Check. Puny paycheck? Yikes. A growing sense of resentment and disillusionment? Done and done. That's all about to change, though. Maybe you've gotten your dream job, or maybe you're relieved to know that it's not a publicist you want to be but a screenwriter, or maybe you just feel grateful not to be as clueless as when you first stepped off that plane at LAX. Yes, these are all accomplishments, each one as significant as the next. Congrats. But, hey, you're not getting off that easy.

You probably don't realize it, but you are standing at a major fork in the road. Down one path is good judgment, a generous spirit, and a strong sense of self. Down the other is greed, selfishness, and cynicism. In screenwriting books they call this the "call to arms" moment. You, dear friends, will accept the challenge.

Take your boss. At one point he stood exactly where you are right now, steadfast in his belief that he would gain success without sacrificing his good sense and decency. "I'll remember what it was like to be poor. I'll call Mom on her birthday. I won't take my assistants for granted. Hell, I'll even refrain from calling them names." But then a little thing called stress rolled his way. His ego, once a sleepy village, quickly expanded into a sprawling suburb, with its own zip code and all. He became "too busy" and "under too much pressure" to worry about little old Mom, let alone the person answering his phones, aka you. So he started asking you to run some personal errands in an effort to save time, then it was making you go to traffic school on his behalf, then it was being expected to nurse him back to health after his biannual bouts of plastic surgery. Suddenly you weren't just his assistant; you were his wife, shrink, and pool boy. (You even measured pH levels each Saturday morning.) The worst part was that the boss found a way to rationalize this as okay behavior. "I pay them. I had to do it once. They should be grateful for the opportunity to learn . . ." It's called a cycle of abuse for a reason, folks. It just goes around and around and . . .

Guess what? The buck stops with you. Each one of us is responsible for sticking to his or her own moral compass. We're here to make sure you do just that.

"And, uh, how?"

May we remind you about all those times when you told yourself you'd never ask your assistant to do your personal errands? Well, then, you can't really make your intern pick up your boyfriend's birthday present at Bloomingdale's, can you? Or remember how upset you got when your boss chose to visit the set instead of his kid's Little League game? Missing your dad's 60th birthday party because there's a really kickass pre-Oscar party the same night is just as bad. Or what about that pact you made with your best friend from home? "I promise, I won't go all Hollywood on you. Blood brothers, for life." Don't you think it's time you return his six-month-old voicemail?

Flash forward 20 years. Now that you've put all our advice to work, chances are you're rich. But we're also guessing (well, hoping) that it wasn't just money that drove you to Hollywood. You wanted to leave your mark on the world, and not just by having your name in some credits. "I don't care if it's a cliché. I will make the world a better place." We're here to remind you of that.

Tutor. Save the manatee. Share some of that bonus with the Boys & Girls Club. Too tied up in work? Then make that work part of your message. Tell your boss that the villain in his new screenplay is a negative stereotype. Convince the studio to turn its next premiere into a charity fundraiser. Option the rights to the book about the poverty-stricken village that everyone says is "too dark." Just don't sit back in your mansion and bask in the glory of your so-called hard work. The potential for movies to change the world is infinite. Be part of it.

FOR FUTURE USE:
HOW TO BE A BETTER BOSS

Follow the below rules to avoid becoming a boss with an assistant who despises you.

P.S. Want to train your current boss? Photocopy this page and post it on the fridge in your office kitchen when nobody's looking.

DO . .

- **Say thank you.** We know, sometimes you'll forget they exist, let alone that they need validation, but a simple thank you can go a long way in making your assistant forget they're fed up with your shenanigans.

- **Buy lunch.** There's nothing worse than watching your boss expense a meal of exotic sushi shipped straight from Tokyo while you're paying $15 for a hot dog from a cart on Wilshire Blvd.

- **Share your bonus.** Sharing is caring, especially when it comes to the noble, hardworking assistants who are dedicating the best years of their lives to making you better at your job. Remember, a little goes a long way, but a lot goes much farther.

- **Give credit where credit is due.** Did your assistant find that article in *The Atlantic Monthly* that became the seed of an idea for a screenplay you set up at the studio? Well, tell people that, or suffer some really bad karma.

- **Allow frequent bathroom breaks.** When's the last time you had to hold it in for longer than is humanly possible? "We're not stopping till Modesto, just hold it, son." Yeah, not a good memory.

DON'T . . .

- **Scream and yell.** Think about it. Taking out your anger on others will not make you get over the trauma that was your childhood. The point: Your assistant is not Mom. Take your anger out on a pillow.

- **Forget their birthday.** Can't remember your assistant's birthday? Then tell them to put it on the calendar in big blinking red letters. Oh, and a present is necessary. A $500 gift certificate to Barneys is standard. A $25 certificate to Jamba Juice is not.

- **Throw things.** Sure, watching your assistant flail as they try to avoid flying phones can be a good source of entertainment, but it's also a sign of weakness. Prove your prowess by practicing restraint.

- **Forget who serves the coffee.** That's right, just like waiters and waitresses everywhere, assistants can also reach the point when they feel justified spitting in your drink.

- **Underestimate the Assistant Corps.** Hell hath no fury like an assistant scorned. Do your assistant wrong and they'll launch a smear campaign that would make even that girl in *The Crucible* blush.

21. The boss thinks you are the greatest thing since Splenda. Still, that doesn't mean he's ready to promote you. In order to get the promotion you . . .

a. keep things status quo, trusting the boss will promote you when he sees fit.

b. work harder, reading every spec and book that has ever been written.

c. start making mistakes so he wants to get you out of there via promotion.

d. threaten to quit if you don't get it.

22. You've worked several assistant jobs now, seen every side of the Biz, and have concluded that this town is a pretty despicable place. You think you'd be happier working as a hygienist back in Sarasota. You . . .

a. put aside the doubt and continue to give in to your ambition.

b. quit your job, take a year off, then return to Hollywood refreshed.

c. settle for a career as a lifetime assistant. Great benefits.

d. hang up the headset and book a flight home.

23. There's a job opening at Fox, but you hate the guy doing the interviews because he slept with your ex-girlfriend. You . . .

a. forget about the job.

b. refuse to apply.

c. apply and use the interview as an opportunity to punch him.

d. let bygones be bygones and pretend like the crime never happened.

24. You've been offered your dream job when you hear about another job opening that is EVEN better. You . . .

a. decide to be grateful for what you have and accept the first job.

b. apply for the second job, hoping that they will call you before you have to accept the other one.

c. apply for the second job, telling them that you have received another offer and need an answer ASAP.

d. turn down the first in the hope that you'll get the second.

25. You have been working for the world's most evil boss for three years when you get an amazing C.E. job at Focus. It's time to tell the evil boss. You . . .

a. march in there with a hot coffee, which you proceed to dump on his toupee before walking out singing.

b. give two days notice and say good riddance. Maybe mace him on the way out.

c. give two weeks notice and help find your replace-ment.

d. give a month's notice, help find a replacement, and tell Dr. Evil that he is the reason you've made it this far.

Answers: 21. c; **22.** d; **23.** d; **24.** c; **25.** d

THAT'S A WRAP!

THAT'S RIGHT, PEOPLE. YOU'VE DONE IT! BY READING THIS BOOK and truly putting into action all the lessons contained herein, you are now that much closer to making your champagne and caviar dreams come true. So get up from the sofa, go to the fridge, and take out that nice cold bottle of bubbly. (It's okay if it's not Cristal. The $14 bottle with an Advil chaser works just as well . . .)

"Toast! Toast!!"

Toast? Okay, we'd love to do that. Everyone raise their glasses. Good. Now it's at this point that we'd like to, well, oh, man . . . Sorry, we didn't think we'd get this emotional. It's just, you all make us so, sob, *prouuuud* . . . Tissues, please.

Seriously, we commend you. Rather than choosing a career that is easy, routine, or safe, you've chosen to follow your calling. It is this gumption, this risk-taking spirit, that will bring you that much closer to success. That said, the road ahead will be difficult. Bosses will yell at you, companies will downsize you, and people will doubt you. Expect that. What you must expect above all else, however, is your ability to press on. To quote Calvin Coolidge, "Nothing in this world can take the place of persistence. Talent will not; nothing is more common than unsuccessful people with talent. Genius will not; unrewarded genius is almost a proverb. Education will not; the world is full of educated derelicts. Persistence and determination alone are omnipotent."

On that note, as sad as it makes us, it's time to let you go. So go. Take what you've learned here, stay focused on the goal, and make success your reality. Dreams—that's what this is all about. Not monetary gain, not expanding the dimensions of your ego, and not the friendship of some B-list celeb. Just some good ol' fashioned dreams.

See you on the red carpet.

A GLOSSARY OF HOLLYWOOD LINGO

20-10-10 Rule The fastest way to read a script. As in, read the first 20 pages, then sample 10 in the middle, and finish up by reading the last 10.

Blind Submission Letter An unsolicited letter to a studio or production company giving an abbreviated pitch for a story idea for a movie. Due to legal reasons, this sort of submission is not accepted by most companies.

Cast and Crew Screening Usually held prior to the world premiere of a movie, this sort of screening lacks the hoopla of a red-carpet opening, but lets the people who actually worked on the movie get a chance to see it without forking over $10.50 at the local Cineplex.

C.E. (Creative Executive) The most entry-level executive position at a production company or studio.

COC (Christmas on Cocaine) The Holidays. In Hollywood. When people have everything and need nothing, a joyride of sin and gluttony can sound like a good idea. It's not.

Cordless Headset A telephone headset that contains a receiver and microphone so the user can move freely about (e.g., to use the bathroom) while simultaneously manning the phones.

Coverage A synopsis and analysis of a script or book used to determine the project's viability for TV or film. Basically, a book report comprised of a 2-to-3-page synopsis, and one page (at most) of comments. It should address the characterizations, dialogue, structure, and overall marketability.

D-Assistant *See* D-Girl.

D-Girl (Development Girl) She reads every script, tracks every deal, and attends every premiere, all with tremendous vigor and ambition. A mogul in training, she usually works at a production company or studio, befriending writers and nosing her way into meetings with the higher-ups. If she's lucky, her diligence and ruthlessness will result in a series of promotions that will end up in her running Fox by the time she's 35.

Drive-on The pass a visitor to the studio will need in order to get past the security guard at the front gate. It's an assistant's job to make sure every visitor on their boss's schedule—the writer, the agent, even Tom Hanks—will have a drive-on waiting for them when they arrive; otherwise they'll be barred from the lot, and this could result in an angry phone call from Tom Hanks himself.

Expense Account The costs incurred while working for the company that are reimbursed to the employee. In the movie business these costs may include meals, drinks, trips, movie tickets, and massages. Lose the receipts and you will suffer the wrath of your boss!

FBJs (Friends Between Jobs) They have either quit or been fired from their assistant jobs and now need money. FBJs make the perfect temps.

FHPP (Future Hollywood Power Player) That's you.

FOF (Friend of a Friend) This is your cousin's mistress's dog-walker. Use her (and others like her) to network and find out about jobs.

Green-light To approve production expenditures and permit the start of principal photography of a film or TV show. This power usually lies with the Studio Chief or the financiers of the film. It'd be way cool to do this someday.

HI MAPs (High Maintenance Peeps) They want and need everything done perfectly, but refuse to do anything themselves. Your boss will most likely be one. ("I wanted the staple three-eighths of an inch from the top, not one-quarter, you heathen!")

HPP (Hollywood Power Player) See Spielberg, Steven, or Mayer, Louis B.

IMDb.com The Internet Movie Database. The go-to source for credits on any actor, director, writer, someday you.

Informational Meeting A meeting with someone in the industry to learn more about his or her specific job and workplace. Not a job interview, per se, but a get-to-know-each-other session.

Internship An unpaid temporary position emphasizing on-the-job experience. You will have to suffer through at least one in order to get your first assistant gig.

J.L., the See UTA Job List.

Lifer A career assistant—as in forever and ever and . . .

Mentor A trusted advisor whom you can turn to for advice and then emulate for the rest of your career. Try to snag one early.

P.A. (Production Assistant) The bottom of the entertainment food chain. One who fetches coffee, photocopies scripts, and runs every type of errand the boss desires. This includes picking up the dry cleaning, shuttling the kids to gymnastics, and cleaning up after the dog.

PCH (The Pacific Coast Highway) A segment of Route 1 in California that you will one day drive between work and your Malibu mansion. Or so you hope.

Phone Sheet A computerized list by which one keeps track of all incoming and outgoing phone calls. Perhaps an assistant's most important possession.

Scene Breakdown Exactly what it sounds like. It's an outline, or breakdown, of every scene in the script. Descriptions of what happens in each scene should be one to two sentences at most.

S.O. (Significant Other) Your boss's girlfriend, boyfriend, husband, wife, or dog—depending on the situation. Treat them all with love, even if your feelings border on the opposite. No one ever got fired for too much brownnosing with the S.O.

Spec A script available for purchase. That is, the writer's agent will send it to buyers and the entire town will read it at once, at which point one of two things will happen. People will say (1) it's the best thing since *Chinatown,* or (2) that it's a product of too much hype and deserves to end up in the recycling bin. Some notorious specs that sold for the big bucks are *Showgirls* (grossed $2M), *The Long Kiss Goodnight* ($4M), and *Lady in the Water* ($5M). We never said anything about price correlating with quality.

Stockholm Syndrome A psychological response seen in hostage situations, in which the hostage shows signs of loyalty to the hostage-taker, regardless of the danger (or at least risk) in which the hostage has been placed. Often seen in assistants with nightmarish bosses.

Swag Promotional items or gifts given away by the studio (e.g., *Shrek* sweatpants, *Superman* key chains, etc.).

Tentpole A studio's big-budget, banner movie for that year, around which the rest of the year's schedule usually revolves. Think *Spider-Man* and *Pirates of the Caribbean*.

Three-Act Structure The most basic rule for structuring the modern screenplay: Give the thing a beginning, middle, and end. Learn it, live it, love it.

TIK (Those in the Know) Celebrities, starlets, club-goers, publicity hounds, etc. Befriend TIK whenever you can.

Tracking Boards Online bulletin boards where young Hollywood hopefuls can trade information about specs, casting updates, and gossip. Frequent several of them in order to impress your boss with your amazing knowledge.

Trades, the The daily, must-read newspapers in the entertainment industry. The big two: *Variety* and the *Hollywood Reporter*.

UTA Job List A list of jobs and internships compiled by the United Talent Agency. Once a highly sought after document, it's now lost its luster due to overexposure and easy accessibility. Also known as the J.L.

Weekend Read The pile of scripts that executives tote home to read (or pretend to read) every weekend. The pile consists of projects by the writers everyone needs to know or the new drafts of projects already in development.

AN INTERVIEW WITH TV'S MOST FAMOUS ASSISTANT

Rex Lee, famous for playing Ari Gold's assistant Lloyd on *Entourage*, was a real-life Hollywood assistant before getting his big break. We gave him a call to get the inside scoop on being an assistant.

Hillary and Peter: You've become the inspiration for thousands of kids who want to make a name for themselves in Hollywood. They literally move here to be Lloyd. Do you think the show gives an accurate portrayal of what's in store for them?

Rex: Certainly. There are a lot of situations I find myself in on the show that remind me of my days as an assistant. In general, just having a boss who is very impatient—asking me to do something and then a few seconds later, asking why it's not done—is very much a part of being a Hollywood assistant. You'd think your boss would give you a realistic amount of time to finish a task, but then there they are a few minutes later, asking you if it's done yet.

H&P: You did what every assistant dreams of doing—making it to the next level. How did your real-life assistant gig help charter the path to becoming TV's most famous assistant?

Rex: I definitely think that being an assistant helped me get the role on *Entourage.* Because of my past jobs, I have a good knowledge of, let's see, what would you call it . . . I guess there's a certain *energy* to being an assistant that I'm familiar with. I've often said that the interesting thing about Hollywood is that most of the players take themselves very, very seriously. Everything is life and death. Because I love Hollywood, and writers, actors, and the business, I think I would buy into that. I would treat my assistant job like it was so important, which was actually an appropriate response. You know, we don't have coolers with donor hearts rushing from hospital to hospital, but everyone still takes it seriously.

H&P: Now that you're a celebrity yourself, how would you recommend assistants deal with you when you come into the office for a meeting? Should they chat you up? Or leave you to peruse the waiting room magazines?

Rex: There are times when I want to be left alone and times when I want to talk to someone. In a perfect world the assistant would be able to read that.

H&P: Did you dream of having an assistant when you were one?

Rex: I never imagined or dreamed that I would have my own assistant. When I was a senior assistant, there were times when I could have bossed other people around. But I was not good at delegating. It was hard for me to see the job other people were doing and think, "Wow, that's so inferior to the job I'm doing." So I'd just do the job myself rather than delegate it to someone else. But I definitely have moments in my life now when I say to myself, "Gosh, I wish I could have an assistant this moment to get this done for me!"

H&P: What's your favorite assistant horror story, on or off the set?

Rex: Well, on the show, I'd have to say it was when Ari asked Lloyd to make himself available . . . sexually. I'm always telling people that our show is tweaked for the sake of comedy, but it can be pretty realistic as well.

H&P: Finally, what words of wisdom would you give a new assistant coming to Ari's firm?

Rex: Do whatever you can to please the boss. Do everything you can to not give me the feeling that you are after my job.

And do look your best.

THANKS

THIS IS OUR FAVORITE PART—HAVING THE CHANCE TO THANK everyone who helped make this book possible. We'd like to start with Tara Mark and Jennifer Unter, whose reminder to "write what you know" made a little writing experiment into this very real book. We are also most grateful to our editors Richard Rosen and Susan Bolotin. It has been an honor to work with people so experienced, funny, smart, supportive, and kind. To everyone at Workman, including, if not especially, the assistants (a special thank you to Randy Lotowycz), your hard work and enthusiasm helped make this an incredible experience. We hope to do it again.

As we're sure you've noticed, this book would not be possible without the many people whose phones we've answered throughout the years. To Amy, Matt, Doug, Lucy, Gail, Rachel, Pete, Laura, Jen, and every agent, exec, and mailroom manager we've ever worked for: We feel honored to have learned from people as talented and hard-working as you.

Equally important in the creation of this project are our incredibly smart, fun, and encouraging coworkers. Thank you for permitting us to take inspiration from so many of our all-night-long-venting-sessions-over-margaritas-at-El-Cholo-because-we-couldn't-afford-therapy. We know that it won't be long before we see each of your faces smiling back at us from the pages of the *Hollywood Reporter's* "Next Generation" issue. Special shout-outs to the amazing Terz, Hannah, Mark, David, Annie K., Jodie, Simran, Alegre, Mary, Sue, Andrew, Anna S., Jessica, Kristen, Lindy, Aggie, Annie L., Elena, Richard, Anna B., Mollie, Andrew, Marla, Ed, George, Eric, Brenda, Claudette, Parry, Lauren, Meghan, Rachel, Amy, the guy at CAA who got us that super-secret script, the girl at the mixer who said she liked our shoes, and that P.A. we saw at the Overland Starbucks with a three-page-long Excel spreadsheet with coffee orders for the entire crew of some movie.

To our amazing brothers and sisters—Tricia, Rich, Lindsay, and Andrew—we are beyond grateful for the many years of laughter, kicks in the butt, and skirmishes over who would get the last pancake. To Jason, who always adored and regulated on us: "Hill and Pete, what the hell is going on? Sell the movie rights already." We'll get back to you on that.

Finally, thank you to the people whose words of wisdom echo throughout this entire book. To Walt, Peg, Betty, and Dick: As parents, you always told us to follow the dream, even the days when the dream looked bleak (e.g., that Saturday night at 1 A.M. copying scripts to send abroad—"Sweetie, it will pay off"). We are proud to be your kids.

AUTHOR BIOS

Peter Nowalk worked as an assistant at an agency, production company, and major studio before scoring his first job as a TV writer. He resides in Los Angeles.

Hillary Stamm was raised in Seattle, Washington. She's currently writing her first novel and working for the chairman of a motion picture studio. She and her husband live in Los Angeles.

Photo Credits